Believe Beyond

"Just because we can't see them doesn't mean they don't exist!"

...Seeing

Debra Martin

Foreword by *Gary E. Schwartz, Ph.D.*

Bloomington, IN

authorHOUSE®

Milton Keynes, UK

AuthorHouse™
1663 Liberty Drive, Suite 200
Bloomington, IN 47403
www.authorhouse.com
Phone: 1-800-839-8640

AuthorHouse™ UK Ltd.
500 Avebury Boulevard
Central Milton Keynes, MK9 2BE
www.authorhouse.co.uk
Phone: 08001974150

This book is a work of non-fiction. However, in select circumstances, the names of people and places have been altered to protect their privacy.

First published by AuthorHouse 8/8/2006

ISBN: 1-4259-5124-4 (sc)

Library of Congress Control Number: 2006906459

Printed in the United States of America
Bloomington, Indiana

This book is printed on acid-free paper.

For Susy Smith,
for believing in me, guiding me, and allowing me
to be a part of her never-ending pursuit of truth

For our loved ones,
who have gone before us
and those left behind,
may we embrace life after death

TABLE OF CONTENTS

FOREWORD

By Gary E. Schwartz, Ph.D.

Professor of Psychology, Medicine, Neurology, Psychiatry and Surgery
Director, Center for Frontier Medicine in Biofield Science
Director, Laboratory for Advances in Consciousness and Health
The University of Arizona

As a scientist, I have chosen to investigate mediumship and the survival of consciousness hypothesis. I have had the privilege (and challenge) to work with some of the world's most gifted and visible mediums–including George Anderson, John Edward, and Allison DuBois–and to document their genuineness in the laboratory. I have witnessed, firsthand, more than twenty different mediums do things that I was taught to believe were "impossible." The research indicates that genuine mediums can see, hear, and/or feel things that most of us typically do not. Debra Martin, the inspired author of this book, has gently–yet convincingly–enabled me to "believe beyond seeing" and appreciate the reality of spirit communication and higher spiritual realms.

Over the years I have learned how to put Yogi Berra's wise words, "If I hadn't believed it, I wouldn't have seen it" into practice. More precisely, I have added essential qualifying words in brackets: "If I hadn't believed it [was possible], I wouldn't have [been open] to see it." As Debra shares with us here, she has learned to cultivate her gift of sensing the often unseen for the beneficent purpose of communicating with departed loved ones, emotional healing, and personal transformation.

I have witnessed Debra participate in experiments where she had received accurate information about an unknown grandmother (known to her granddaughter, but unknown to the world—as featured on the Arts and Entertainment documentary *Mediums: We See Dead People*), and also received equally accurate information about an extraordinarily well known mother and public spokesperson (Princess Diana). In these "single-blind" experiments, Debra was not told the identity of the sitters or the deceased, and she was not allowed to speak with the sitters during the research portion of the readings.

More remarkably, Debra has participated successfully in a "triple-blind" experiment. Not only were the experimenter and the medium both "blind" to the identity of the deceased individuals ("double-blind"), but the sitters were not present at the time their readings occurred making them "blind" as well. They were also "blind" at the time they scored two readings (one was theirs, and the other was a matched control—which makes the experiment "triple-blind"). *The Truth about Medium* book describes this experiment in detail.

Yes, Debra is the "real deal"—a genuine medium—but she is more than this. She is a caring mother, a devoted wife, and a successful businessperson as well as a deeply spiritual and visionary person. What has inspired me most about Debra is her code of ethics. As described in Chapter Eight "Science and Skepticism," Debra is committed to the following ways of living: integrity, truth, compassion, honesty, fairness, ethicality, responsibility, cooperation, spiritual values, respect, and love. It is difficult to be in Debra's presence and not smile.

According to Debra, she found her way to our afterlife research program because of the late Susy Smith—a woman who has participated in multiple experiments in our laboratory since her passing—came to Debra and persisted in bringing her to me. Debra chose to dedicate *Believe Beyond Seeing* to Susy. If Debra is correct—and our research justifies that we give Debra the benefit of the doubt here—we can thank Susy for not only recruiting Debra for research, but for playing a role as Debra's "guide" and possibly "editor" of this book.

Debra is a role model for appreciating the adventure of the "never-ending pursuit of truth" [her words] and the joy of "embracing life after death." There is much to learn and celebrate in this book.

A Message from the Author

When you read my book, I hope that you will reflect upon the following:

> *I would rather live my life as if a wondrous afterlife exists than to live my life believing in no afterlife at all—just dust to dust—only to pass away and discover I was immensely wrong.*

I do not consider this wishful thinking. On the contrary, I have felt, touched, and heard spirits from the other side re-connect with their loved ones here. Based on my experience, which includes participating in controlled scientific experiments, life goes on and on. I truly believe that we will all survive our physical deaths and that each consciousness will continue to exist in another spiritual realm.

This book is about my experiences as a medium. It details how I arrived at my beliefs regarding life, death, and the spiritual world that divides us. It should be noted that I am not a writer *per se*; rather, I wrote this book at the strong encouragement from the scientists at the VERITAS Research Program at the University of Arizona where I volunteer as a medium. In addition, my friends, family, and clients have asked me repeatedly about my experiences and views regarding this subject matter. They, too, encouraged me to tell my story and write about my experiences.

The goal of my book is to share various stories so readers will be compelled to open their mind, heart, and soul to the spirit world. I want this book to provide guidance and comfort to those that have lost loved ones. I can only hope that after reading my book, every reader will become more aware of their interconnection with others–both in this life and the afterlife–so they can see and validate the signs sent from their loved ones. **Truly, if my book only touches one person in this light, then I know I did not write it in vain.**

With that said, my book commences with the story of a little girl named Odessa. I chose to start the book with her because my time with her and her family was so powerful. In fact, she continues to send me signs to this very day. Odessa's spirit comes through to not only her friends and family, but she even got the attention of my writing partner more than once–and to us all, these encounters were not merely coincidences. The signs were more than that.

The next three chapters chronicle how I realized that I had an extraordinary gift, how I learned to use and channel my gift in various ways, and how I became involved with the VERITAS Research Program. Again, it was not a coincidence. As you will read, a very influential spirit named Susy Smith guided me persistently and convincingly to the University of Arizona and there has been no turning back. **I am fortunate to participate with an incredible team of experts that give validation to my life's work and me.** Their scientific studies and documented research provide a solid foundation for me to pursue my gift and say to the skeptics, "This is not nonsense. The VERITAS team has collected hard evidence supporting life after death and has concluded the soul continues eternally."

Next, I will take you through the process of dying via a dear friend. We were together here in this world, and then he touched me from the other side. I will continue to share with you various stories about loved ones who received what I call "Messages from Above." For some, there is no greater gift.

From there, I will address how I view psychic predictions and then discuss science versus skepticism. I will walk you through a typical reading. I will share my Code of Ethics as a medium. I will explain the process of a triple-blind reading and how these sort of research experimentations, when done with success, point directly to another world.

The last chapters are especially dear to my heart as they address two topics. The first is suicide. I will address suicide and my perspective on what happens to the soul of a person who suffers from a suicide. I chose to include this chapter because I was a victim of suicide and there was little written on this topic by mediums. I will conclude with a chapter titled "Connected." In it, I will share the tragic story of a high school car accident, the loved ones that were touched, and the circle of life that was epitomized.

Finally, I included Personal Validations taken directly from letters I received from clients. They all graciously agreed to share their stories with you, the reader. These stories are written from their hearts and provide valuable feedback to not only me as a medium, but possibly to you.

Simply stated, after reading my book, I sincerely hope that your soul will be awakened so you can imagine the vast possibilities that could be waiting for you on the other side.

✛ 1 ✛

<u>Odessa</u>

ON FRIDAY MORNING, OCTOBER 1, 2004, I had butterflies in my stomach. I was giving a reading to a family who had lost their daughter. I was not told her age or how she died. I was given only her name–Odessa. This family sought from me a sense of peace, and I wanted to prove to them that their daughter was still very much alive.

Julie Beischel, Ph.D. referred Odessa's family to me. Dr. Beischel is the Assistant Director of VERITAS, a research program of the Human Energy Systems Laboratory in the psychology department at the University of Arizona. VERITAS Director Gary Schwartz, Ph.D. and Dr. Beischel study mediums, like myself, to test the hypothesis that the consciousness (or identity) of a person survives physical death.[1]

As part of her research, Dr. Beischel joined Odessa's mother, father, and maternal grandparents at my home that Friday morning.

"I want you to know your daughter Odessa is here," I said as I led them into my home office. I handed Odessa's mother, Anita, a gray, white-tipped feather about four inches long. "When I looked to see if you had arrived, I noticed this feather outside of my front door. I have never before seen a feather at my doorstep, and I knew Odessa had placed it there–a little sign to me that the reading would go well and that I

1

should not worry. Birds are very special to Odessa." Odessa's mother and grandmother exchanged glances with guarded curiosity.

I also noticed that Anita was pregnant. I said, "I hear from Odessa that you're having a little girl." Anita smiled and replied, "Yes, you're right."

The family sat on the sofa and chair in my office while I sat on the floor facing them. To start, I briefly explained how I conducted my sessions. Prior to a reading, I sit quietly with the spirit and take notes on the images, words, and feelings the spirit gives me. I explained that in addition to offering this precedent information, the spirit also communicates with me during the reading itself. I pointed out, however, that the spirit's information has no meaning to me. I was merely a messenger. I then handed the family two-and-half pages of typed notes that I had taken from Odessa and told them that they would have to determine the significance of Odessa's words, a bit like putting puzzle pieces together.

We began with the notes' first paragraph. The image was a car wreck on a slippery road, an accident that happened quickly, without time to correct. I said to them, "Odessa conveyed to me lots of sadness, even from herself, and her puzzlement at the loss of control. Odessa gave me the image of her own hand on her forehead."

The family did not comment. I moved onto a paragraph about "lemon trees," words Odessa said were from a conversation the family had that day in the car. "She has been in the car with you the entire time," I said.

At this point, Anita laid her typed sheets on the coffee table and sat back on the sofa. "This is not my daughter," she stated with a swallowed sob. "Odessa is not here today."

I was stunned. In my heart, I knew these were Odessa's words.

"Odessa did not die in a car accident," Anita explained. "We don't have lemon trees…" The grandmother gently interrupted her daughter and explained that the family discussed *citrus* trees in the car on the way to the reading, but Anita had not heard because she was in a phone conversation with Dr. Schwartz at the time. This explanation pacified Anita somewhat. I added that the car wreck might have been intended as a symbol of accidental death, rather than the literal cause of death. She nodded quietly and agreed to continue.

Just one paragraph down, I had recorded that Odessa was very careful with her words around me because she said her mother "would analyze what is said to pieces." The family chuckled at this well-timed observation, and the grandmother interjected, "Now I *know* this is Odessa. Boy, has she got her mother pegged!"

We continued through my notes. Much of what I wrote was considered a "hit," a term the VERITAS researchers used to define information that was accurate and pertinent to a spirit or to his or her family.

Odessa also mentioned her grandmother's "beautiful, yummy, chocolate cakes." The grandmother acknowledged that she often baked a vanilla cake with chocolate icing. She said that she usually decorated it with fresh flowers, which drew praise from family and friends.

Next, Odessa referred to "burnt toast," and when I shared this with the family, they burst out laughing. Anita explained that Odessa's grandmother had a habit of burning the bread when she cooked a meal.

Odessa noted the name "Jackson," one of two specific names she gave me. Anita explained that Jackson was a friend about Odessa's age, who was more like a cousin to Odessa. Anita said she was impressed at the mention of his name since it was an uncommon one.

Despite hits like these, I could tell Anita was still skeptical and disappointed as the reading ended. Part of her skepticism, Anita later explained, came from the age-appropriateness of the images and words alleged to be Odessa's. Remember, I did not know Odessa's age, and based on her communication ability, I was under the impression that she was sixteen years old. Anita later told me that Odessa was, in fact, just thirteen months old when she died. My misperception provided a good example of the discrepancy between a spirit's age at time of death and his or her communication abilities in the afterlife.

If clients come to a reading with expectations of what they want to hear, they risk disappointment. I still felt challenged by this family to prove what I do is real, but I trusted in Odessa's spirit. A spirit had never let me down before, so why would one now? I also have a policy never to end a reading unless my clients feel complete peace knowing that we have truly spoken with their loved one.

I somehow needed to touch this woman. I offered her a one-on-one reading, in private, by chance she and Odessa could communicate more openly. I hoped this would provide that sense of peace the group reading had failed to deliver. She welcomed the opportunity, and Dr. Beischel agreed that this portion would remain off research records.

I later learned that as I led Anita to another room for the private reading, she was silently asking Odessa for a sign that I could be trusted. Anita then asked me if she could use the bathroom before our reading continued. I directed her down the hall. Anita told me later that she kept talking to Odessa, "Just show her a horse, baby. Show her a horse." Odessa, I later learned from Dr. Beischel, died after a horse kicked her in the head as she sat on her mother's hip. The mention of a horse, Anita felt, would be good proof Odessa's spirit was truly here. As Anita walked into the bathroom, she turned to see a 32x40 inch painting of horses dominating the small room. She chuckled and said to Odessa, "Okay! I got it! I'll try to be open."

Since this reading was one-on-one, Anita and I sat facing each other and holding hands. I could hear Odessa saying "mama" with the inflection she used when she was alive. I repeated what I heard and then explained to Anita that I could feel Odessa using my body as a vessel for her own movements. "Odessa likes to dance," I said, "but . . . it's more of a bobbing up and down." I chuckled as my body began simulating Odessa's movements. "Yes!" Anita said. "That's exactly how she danced!" Odessa had truly arrived, and so had her mother's trust in me. We both began to cry. The reason this reading required privacy became clear–Anita was able to share her feelings without worrying about their effect on her family.

Odessa again showed me something furry and white in her room. She had given me this image during the group reading, but it had stumped everyone. Odessa was persistent. I offered suggestions: "A cat? A blanket? A rug?" Anita shook her head. Then, Odessa showed me it could wrap over her shoulders. "Her white fur coat!" Anita exclaimed.

Anita was amazed and amused. "She only wore it once, for Christmas Eve," she said while shaking her head. "I didn't think it was that important to her. It was an impractical purchase, but I bought it for her because, as I told her, 'you only live once.'" I heard Odessa exclaiming, "Yes! Yes! Yes! You've got it!" Odessa was showing her mother the coat because she wanted to return its message. She wanted her mother to keep living *her* life to the fullest. I told Anita that she could feel Odessa's energy when she touched the coat and that Odessa meant it to be saved as a token from her. Odessa also made it clear that she did *not* want to share the coat with her unborn sister. Anita and I chuckled. I felt that Odessa's true spirit had finally come out.

At the end of our private reading, Odessa said she would send a small, yellow-bellied, chirpy bird as a sign that she was around. She told her mother, "The baby bird represents that I am still your baby and I always will be. Nothing changes just because I have crossed over. Talk to me, I hear you, and I will respond to let you know I am always by your side."

The next morning, the little bird revealed itself. Anita and her family were staying at a guest ranch in Tucson. While Anita sat on the patio outside of her cabin and journaled her experience, a little chirpy bird with a yellow belly landed in the tree next to her. It sat there while she finished her entry. For the next two days of her stay, she never saw it again.

Prior to their flight home, Odessa's family discovered what seemed to be another gift from Odessa. They were meeting Dr. Beischel for a farewell dinner at a Phoenix restaurant, and as they walked up to the front door, the grandmother stooped to pick up a small brown feather, very much like the one left at my doorstep. "Oh look," she said, handing the feather to Anita, "Odessa left us another feather." Anita said she was hesitant to think too much of it at the time, but not wanting to discourage her mother's hope, she nodded and smiled. She placed the feather next to her setting at the table. When Dr. Beischel arrived and took her seat across from Anita, she asked, "So what's with the feather?" When Anita told her the story, Dr. Beischel smiled and exclaimed, "Well, there's my answer!"

Dr. Beischel explained that she had been struggling all day to find appropriate graphics for the VERITAS homepage. Dr. Schwartz had suggested a "white crow" to correlate with the lab's signature quote by William James, MD:

> *If you wish to upset the law that all crows are black,*
> *you mustn't seek to prove that no crows are; it is enough*
> *to prove one single crow to be white.*

Dr. Beischel could not find any graphics of a white crow that suited her, so she was considering the idea of using a series of black feathers and one white one. Again, Odessa's timing appeared appropriate, this time for more than one party.

Later that month, another feather appeared. I asked my website designer to scan Odessa's pictures onto my computer and shared with her Odessa's story. She then told me that same morning she woke to find a feather inside of her house by the front door. She showed it to me, and it looked just like the one I found on my own doorstep. I believe it was Odessa's way of saying thank you.

✦　✦　✦

My relationship with Odessa continued to develop. Four months later, I sat in a hotel room in Seattle, writing the first draft of this chapter. I had joined my husband, Ric, on a business trip and used my time alone to write. I placed Odessa's picture on the hotel room desk and asked her for guidance as I wrote her story. Before I began, however, Odessa asked if we could buy her newborn sister, Arabella, a gift. She wanted an angel. I thought, "Odessa, we are in a hotel in downtown Seattle. How are we going to find an angel?" Odessa told me to trust her. I agreed to her request, but told her I must write first.

At midday, I was wrapping up when Ric invited me to join him for lunch. When I arrived in the lobby, I noticed a shadow box displaying gift items for sale in a shop across the street. Inside this box was a fairy. Emotion overcame me at the sight of it, and I knew Odessa was guiding me there.

After lunch, I visited the store but found no angels. I looked up and then noticed a fairy, like the kind displayed at the hotel, hanging by fishing line from the ceiling. "That's the one," Odessa said to me. The sales clerk said she had no more of that particular fairy, so I asked her to take the last one down and wrap it up for me.

I went directly to the post office and mailed the package to Arabella. Enclosed with the fairy was the following message I wrote from Odessa:

> *Whenever you feel alone or afraid, please know that I am here for you.*

At the end of the message, I added Odessa's instructions that the fairy be hung in Arabella's room and be considered an angel.

I called to tell Anita this story, and when the package arrived a few days later, I received the following email from her. She wrote:

> *We received Odessa's angel. It is perfect. I want to share with you how appropriate it is—Odessa's room was decorated with fairies and we've incorporated those fairies into Arabella's room. The artist who designed most of the fairy artwork and figurines we're using is Cicely Mary Barker, the same artist of the Flower Fairy you sent. When I opened your package and saw Odessa's fairy, I couldn't believe it!*

Spirits come to us in many ways. Some provide tangible signs such as Odessa's feathers or fairies, while others appear through a familiar scent such as a favorite perfume, a fresh-cut rose, or a tobacco pipe. Regardless of the form, these signs become our unique connection with our loved ones. Pay attention. Walk with your eyes open. These phenomena are not imagined. Spirits protect, guide, and love us. Your loved one may have passed into the afterlife, but they walk with you daily. Odessa still is very much alive. She has continued to leave feathers for her family, and Anita said that little yellow-bellied birds have appeared to her at appropriate moments when she needed to know Odessa was near.

I am continually amazed by the amount of trust I have in spirits as well as by their abilities to guide me. I want to thank Odessa for using me as her vessel for communication. She has allowed me to give her parents experiences they will treasure forever. I will always cherish that October reading in 2004. My relationship with Odessa will never end. I love the Odessa that I know now as a spirit child, and I look forward to meeting her when I cross over.

✛ ✛ ✛

While my writing partner, Michelle Madruga, was editing the draft of this chapter, she told me that she thought a lot about Odessa and Arabella. She wondered how their family chose their names. What did their names mean? Were the girls alike? Or were they different? These notions ran through Michelle's head repeatedly.

The next morning, Michelle was shopping for Christmas stockings for her family. While at a store, she was drawn to its children's section. She flipped through a few books and then pulled out a nicer book titled *Arabella* by Wendy Orr.[2] She stood there in disbelief. Nearly twelve hours earlier, only Odessa and Arabella were on her mind. What were the odds of finding a book with such a unique name? She went to put it back but then knew she had to purchase it for Odessa's family.

Michelle arrived home and confirmed that the baby's name was spelled exactly like the book's title. She then left me the following message: "I have a story for you about Arabella. A coincidence? You tell me..."

I called her immediately. "I can understand if the title was an ordinary name," Michelle said, "like Samantha or Cindy, but Arabella?" I told her that it was not a coincidence. Odessa was trying to send a message to her family once again. I applauded Michelle for having an open mind and heart, but more importantly, for her willingness to act upon her instincts and purchase the book.

Beyond the title, the book's story seemed to carry significance. The story centered around a model ship named *Arabella*. It was a grandpa's most prized possession because "she'll always stay to bring me luck." One night, a storm broke the window in which the model sat and blew it out to sea. Unbeknownst to the grandpa, his young grandson risked his life in the storm to find it because "Grandpa would never be happy without his *Arabella*." Upon the grandson's return, the grandpa exclaimed, "I thought I'd lost what I love best in all the world!" "The Arabella?" the grandson asked. "You," said the grandpa.

The *Arabella* model is not a direct symbol of Odessa's sister, Arabella, since the ship rates below the grandson in importance. But the story itself reflects Odessa's family's feelings—that nothing is more important to them than the life of their children.

When I told Anita about Michelle's experience, she was grateful Michelle had the open and generous heart to purchase the book on her behalf. She said that she and her family would always treasure the book and the story of how it came to be theirs.

With respect to Michelle, Odessa was not yet through. Only two days later, on Michelle's way to meet her husband for lunch with their children, a van switched lanes right in front of her. Written on the van was, "ADESA Golden Gate." She called me again and said, "Maybe I'm reading into it?" She added, "Could it really be another coincidence? Again, what were the odds?" The names were too unique to be a coincidence. Although the spelling was different, the company was based in the same city as her husband's work. I told her that the van was Odessa's way of thanking her for the book.

✦   ✦   ✦

Odessa

I give my heartfelt thanks to Anita Webster, Odessa's mother, for her editing and contributions to this chapter.

✦ 2 ✦

<u>My Near Death Experiences</u>

MY FIRST ENCOUNTER WITH A NEAR DEATH EXPERIENCE occurred on August 31, 1997. It was the same night Princess Diana passed away in that infamous Paris car crash. Like Princess Diana, I was also in a car accident that night, but thankfully, my outcome was different.

I was with two girlfriends, Lisa and Sheri, at a restaurant/sports pub. During our conversation, one of the bar televisions flashed a news bulletin that Princess Diana had passed away and then reiterated that fateful event. After the news segment, anxiety overcame me. I felt very strange, like something bad was going to happen to me too. Even so, I did not mention this trepidation to my girlfriends. Instead, I talked myself out of it and figured it was all in my mind because of what we had just witnessed on the news.

Unfortunately, my premonition proved true. That is, on our way home, I sat in the backseat of Lisa's small sports car. Lisa drove, and Sheri was the frontseat passenger. While we were driving in the slow lane on Highway 60 in Phoenix, Arizona, we heard a big bang. We were hit forcefully by another car, yet none of us saw it coming. I prayed in my head, "Please help us! This is not our time!" Sheri and I were both single mothers with three young children each. Who would take care of them if something happened to us?

Our car spun at least four times, taking out forty feet of guardrail. An extended white van with no windows along its side hit us. The van came from the fast lane. Because the driver was not paying attention, he almost missed his exit. To compensate, he veered across multiple lanes. He hit us without ever seeing we were there. In turn, he flipped his van three times off the side of the highway.

Our car finally came to a stop, but we were not out of harm's way. We were left facing oncoming traffic, and the three of us were stuck in the car. Before we could panic, a Good Samaritan arrived to help us out of the car. He was a gentleman of African descent. He helped Sheri first and then myself. He helped us away from the highway and sat us on the hillside. He then carried Lisa and placed her closer to the car because her leg was broken. There was no one else around.

After we were all safely away from the car, the gentleman approached me to see if I was okay. I told him that my finger was injured. In the accident, my silver ring had bent into my finger, causing it to bleed profusely. Without hesitation, this man put my bleeding finger into his mouth and re-bent the ring with his teeth. He then removed it from my finger and handed it back to me. He kissed me on the forehead and told me that I would be fine. He said that I would see him again someday. He also said this to my two friends.

At that moment, I could hear the sirens coming for us. They were in the distance on my right. The man then walked past me, on my left. After a brief moment, I turned to look for him, but he was gone. Lisa and Sheri did not see him either. After the ambulance arrived, we asked the paramedics if they had seen him, but they had not. No one else saw him but the three of us. There were no other witnesses.

Based only on what I knew at the time, I believed that he was an angel sent to us in human form. He came down for the sole purpose of divine intervention that night. I still have my ring with his teeth marks embedded.

If I were to put all of my body weight on the ring, the metal of this ring would not bend. It truly amazes me, and I look at it with awe. This ring serves as a reminder of how lucky we were that night, but more importantly, the ring is a symbol of truth that someone helped us when we needed it most. It is truly a profound validation that it was not our imaginations that night.

It took months for all of us to heal from this accident. I am grateful that we all came out of this accident with no permanent injuries. As for the man who hit us, he too was lucky. He was not seriously harmed in any way.

✦   ✦   ✦

Soon after the accident, I began researching angels and the afterlife. It perplexed me that Lisa, Sheri, and I all witnessed a man who helped us with the utmost of kindness, but then appeared to have vanished. I knew in my heart he must have been an angel, but for logic's sake, I wanted to find an explanation.

As such, I attended a Doreen Virtue seminar a few months later. Ms. Virtue is a very famous spiritual clairvoyant known around the world for her work with angels. Clairvoyant means one can see spirits, symbols, objects, colors, and even visions into one's future. I went to an angel therapy workshop with my close friend Jan as well as Sheri from the accident.

That day, Ms. Virtue taught us to hear our angels' names. We all sat quietly on the floor of a conference room that held approximately one hundred people. Before we began, we needed to clear our "Chakras." The body has seven spinning energy centers that look like spinning wheels. Chakra means "wheel" in Sanskrit. Once our minds, hearts, and ears were clear and open, we asked our angels to speak their names to us. We heard and saw their individual responses in our own minds.

Sheri told us that she clearly heard a male angel's voice. He told her that his name was Jamal. She then could see that he was of African descent. After Sheri told us about her angel, we exchanged glances in disbelief. Without saying a word to each other, we both knew that it was Jamal, Sheri's angel, who saved us from that frightful accident.

I heard three angels, but one in particular stood out. Her name was Giselle. Giselle stood in front of me that day, and continues to do so. I ask her for guidance, especially when I feel lost. I know that she is always with me because I often feel her presence. I believe that she will never leave me. I know that she guides me even when I am unaware. I also believe that she has been with me since the day I was born and will be with me until I die. In addition, I also ask other guides and angels to assist me when I need them. As I grow in the spiritual world, I believe that I will meet more throughout my lifetime.

During the workshop, I also envisioned being handed a microphone. Jan saw a football bleacher filled with people waiting for me to speak. We were unsure if the people we saw were living or from the afterlife. In retrospect, it was as if I was given a microphone to symbolize the voice I would use as a medium between spirits and their loved ones.

Finally, Jan heard her angel's name. It was Anita. Jan was handed a heart during her private meditation. The symbolism of a heart for Jan was appropriate because she gave hers to many people being a hospice caretaker. Being single, Jan interpreted this heart as the love she had desired for so long. Today, she is in a loving relationship.

As our meditations progressed that day, Sheri envisioned receiving a tape recorder. We joked that she would tape me talking with the microphone. However, the tape recorder proved appropriate. Since the accident, Sheri began attending more workshops and seminars relating to the afterlife. As a result, she developed a business around it. Specifically, she began audio taping spiritual speakers as a business and then sold the tapes during their seminars.

✦   ✦   ✦

About five years later, Sheri was taping an event called the Conscious Living Expo. It was held in the state of Washington. While walking around to meet some of the speakers, she was drawn to a clairvoyant boy about twelve years old. He was there as part of the expo to meet with individuals. Sheri anxiously asked the clairvoyant child what he could read about her.

Amongst other key comments, he told Sheri that she had been in a terrible car accident with two friends. He told her that she and her friends were all saved by divine intervention. He then reiterated accurate events from the evening. Specifically, he said that an angel had come down in human form and helped them away from the accident. He told her that she would meet him again and then confirmed his name. He too called him Jamal. This was the second time a spiritual clairvoyant validated this information—what were the odds?

After Sheri returned from the expo and relayed the story to me, I reflected back on the accident and other spiritual happenings in my life. I was quite certain that I had some unusual, supernatural gift. But what it was and how I could develop it, I had no idea where to begin. Quite frankly, I was overwhelmed and scared. The only thing that I knew for sure was that it was an incredible gift to know that angels could help us when we asked them and needed it most.

I did more research on the Internet, at bookstores, and in libraries. I also attended more seminars. The accumulation of the accident, the clairvoyant child, and Ms. Virtue's seminar made me, as well as Jan and Sheri, certain that it was not all summed up as a coincidence. As a result, we started meditating as a group once per week. We wanted to see what would happen, if anything, when we called on our angels and spirits ourselves.

We sat on the floor and practiced hearing from the afterlife. Each of us would say what we saw and heard during these meditations. Although exciting at first, it was also scary because we were in an unknown territory. We agreed to continue because it was important for us to appreciate what happened at the accident and at the spiritual seminars thereafter.

During our mediations, we validated each other's messages and shared what we saw or heard. Sometimes one would receive more information than another would, so we would piece together our messages. It seemed to be clear, purposeful, and powerful. Week after week, there was no doubt in our minds that these spirits had something to say, and they felt that they could do it through us. But what was I supposed to do with this? How was I going to develop this skill? More importantly, why did they choose me?

We also discovered that each one of us had a similar spirit that was once a living family member from generations back. These spirits would be present during each of our meditations. What made it interesting was the fact that we were only able to see each other's spirits, but not our own. For example, Jan was able to see my father sitting on the stairs watching us; however, I could not. It was not until later that I was able to see my father.

✦   ✦   ✦

It was shortly thereafter that my second near death experience took place. It occurred on August 30, 2000. My husband Ric had proposed to me the night before. I was elated.

While driving to a friend's home, I was sitting in a left turn bay waiting for traffic to clear. Out of nowhere, a mid-size car hit me from behind. It did not even slow to avoid me. Before I could process what was happening, a very clear voice asked me, "Are you ready?" I replied defiantly, "No, I am not ready! My life is too good right now!"

My car came to a stop in oncoming traffic. My car was a four-door Honda Accord, but became more like a two-door accordion. A gentleman, who was experiencing seizures and driving erratically, hit me full force. The police were in pursuit but unable to stop him in time. He rammed right into my back end, at over 50 miles per hour. Due to the force, my seat belt broke. I landed in what was left of my backseat and with a mouth full of glass.

While I was unconscious, I witnessed the scene of the accident via an out of body experience. I saw, as if from above, all that was going on. I was with someone, was it an angel? Or God? Or another divine form? I could not see him, but I could converse with him and knew that he was by my side. Next, I clearly saw that my car was going to be struck again, this time by a very large truck. It was crystal clear, like a movie playing over and over in my head.

It was then that I returned to my body. I regained consciousness and was climbing back into the frontseat when two men approached me. One of the men was trembling and visibly shaken up. I heard him tell the other gentleman that he was pulling a trailer full of tractors with his truck. He said that he did not know what happened, but it was as if someone grabbed his steering wheel away from him and pulled him into oncoming traffic. He said that he would have driven right over my car and me had that not happened. Amazingly, he did not hit anyone, nor was he injured.

After the man finished his story, I immediately realized that I had seen these pending events from above–before they ever happened. I saw the truck about to hit me, but due to divine intervention, once again, the truck was steered away. Clearly, my choice to come back to life influenced the direction of this truck. It was not my time to cross over. I still had my three children to care for, and now a fiancée with whom to share my life. I could not have been more blessed, now a second time.

After my out of body experience, I knew more than ever that there was an afterlife. Hovering over the car wreck and watching the sequence of events unfold was all incredibly real. More importantly, I was given a choice to continue living or to cross over. The voice that asked me this life-changing question still resonates in my head. Fortunately, I walked away from it all without any significant injuries. I had to undergo several months of treatment for my lower back, a very small price to pay for my life.

Based on the first accident, the spiritual seminars, the meditations and now this second accident, I finally believed I knew how I needed to use my gift. I was convinced I came back to life for a specific purpose. That purpose was to connect people in this world with their loved one in the afterlife. I knew that it sounded like a lofty goal. However, because I seemed to connect with the spirits so well, I figured it was worth a shot to be their messenger. How else could one explain these miraculous circumstances in my life?

Once I gave into the spirits and resigned myself to this new purpose, I remembered spiritual incidents from my childhood. When I was a child, I saw faces in the dark while I lay in bed. I thought that these faces were looking at me. Given my youth, this scared me, and I fought going to bed nearly every night. Not surprisingly, I was also too afraid to tell anyone what I was seeing.

These faces wanted to talk with me. They knew that I could hear them, but because I was too young to understand, I consistently tuned them out. So much so, I forgot that this ever happened until this extraordinary sequence of events in my life.

I also believe that I was born with this gift. It is now clear to me that my father had the gift, and now I know that two of my four children do as well. Because my children are still young, they have not acted on their gifts yet, and may never. I do know that my father did. After my mother passed away, he told me that while he was driving in his car, she came to him. He could hear and see her. She was healthy and happy. They were able to converse as if she had never passed. Because this happened well before any of these aforementioned events, I did not accept what my father shared with me as being valid and dismissed it. As a result, I never knew if he spoke with my mother again.

Moreover, I also believe that everything happens for a reason. I turned the spirits away in my childhood, but they knew when the time was right, I would let them in and listen. I am grateful to them that they were so patient with me. As established in Chapter One, I am now able to let the spirits use me as their messenger to communicate with their grieving loved ones.

The key to my success was practice, practice, and more practice. I spent hours listening to the spirits. I spent more time in the library and on the Internet. I spent time with other mediums, listening and learning from them. I attended more seminars. All of these elements, combined with the support from my family and friends, allowed me to become a viable means for which spirits and loved ones could re-connect.

Every reading I do is special and never forgotten. I believe each spirit leaves a thumbprint on my heart. I am never scared. The spirits contact me out of love for their loved ones. I have never had any spirit come through with a malicious intent. I am not surprised, since my underlying purpose is based on love. In fact, many of the spirits remain friends, and I talk with them frequently. Like my friends and family here on earth, they give me support and guidance. Without them, I would be lost because they have become an integral part of my life.

For those of you who think you may have this gift of hearing the spirits from the afterlife, my advice is to practice as much as possible. Just like any talent, the more practice you have, the keener your skills become.

Finally, it is worth noting that there are many types of mediums available for guidance. Mediums are unique and have their own special gift. Before you see one, be careful to do sufficient research to insure this person meets your needs, and above all, is reputable and established in the spiritual world.

✦3✦

Healings

HEALERS REQUIRE AN INCREDIBLE AMOUNT OF ENERGY in order to be effective. For me, I must put all of my trust into my guides, angels, and the Highest Divine in hopes of helping another individual overcome his or her ailment. I must wholeheartedly concentrate and connect with my guides in order to direct the ill person or their family. Based on my research, healers seem to have their own techniques. One is not necessarily better than another is. It all depends on what has proved most effective for that particular healer.

When I discovered that I had a gift for connecting with the afterlife, I did not realize healing would be a part of it. Instead, it became a natural progression because I could connect with the afterlife. The same angels, guides, spirits, and Highest Divine that I called on for my readings were also capable of guiding me to help ill persons, or their families in need.

However, it is important to note that in every healing situation, I am only present to serve as a vessel of communication. That is, I allow the spirits to guide me in hopes of bringing peace to either the ill person or the loved ones. Ultimately, the outcome of my healing services is what is meant to be from above. *I cannot stress this point enough.* We healers are simply facilitators to connect those in need on earth with the ultimate powers from above.

✛   ✛   ✛

Before I perform a healing, I ask my guides, angels and the Highest Divine for protection. I want them to protect me from the negative energy that continues to exist in the afterlife as well as from the illness that I am healing so I do not expose myself to it. I only want to be surrounded with good and positive energies. Next, I ask for assistance from the following angels and repeat their respective prayers:

> *Archangel Raphael, guide me to all the areas that need to be healed giving my hands healing energy.*
>
> *Archangel Michael, give me the strength to heal in all areas.*
>
> *Archangel Gabriel, allow me to hear what I need to do and then give me the words that I need to say.*
>
> *Archangel Uriel, allow me to do this with total peace and love.*
>
> *The Highest Divine, I allow You to use me as Your vessel. I trust that what is about to happen is under Your total control.*

I developed this prayer after reading Doreen Virtue's book, *Angel Therapy*.[3] Based on my experiences, I found that these angels as a group have been most effective for me. Again, since each circumstance is unique, I may also be guided to bring in other angels or guides for assistance in a healing.

At the end of a healing, I pray that the Highest Divine surrounds my clients with a white light. I pray that this heavenly light surrounds them, as if it were a tornado inside of them, from head to toe. I want it to touch every organ, every vessel, and every cell in their body. Once I see this white light, I know there is nothing more I can do. I then feel a peace from above and know that my services are complete.

Again, since I work only as the messenger, I ensure that my clients understand upfront that whatever the outcome of my healing services may be, the true blessings come from the Highest Divine. You will see this clearly demonstrated in the following healings.

Albert

First, I will tell you a story about my son's best friend. His name is Albert. Both Albert and my son, Steven, were attending their last year of high school in 2003. The two boys were always together and seemed to walk around with no cares in the world. In fact, Albert often joined our family for Sunday breakfast.

Given the amount of time spent at our home, Albert and I developed a close bond. He was always interested in my work, particularly how I would use energy in my hands. Once, I showed him how to receive energy when he was tired. As I explained, he first needed to rub his hands together briskly until they became warm. I then told him to place his palms over his closed eyes for a few minutes. After the energy (warmth) drained from his hands, he should feel rejuvenated–and he did.

Albert had great trust in me and deeply respected what I did. One could describe Albert as an exceptionally caring soul. He came from a divorced family. The most important people in his life were his mother and his siblings. Because he was the oldest son, he assumed a role of responsibility. He would do anything to help his family either financially or emotionally. He was an exceptional teenager, one who had to grow up too fast.

It was July 2003, the summer after graduation, and I wondered if the celebration would ever end. Soon thereafter, Albert and his girlfriend from seventh grade broke up. He had difficulty in accepting this break up, especially when it became unpleasant.

Albert shared with me rumors that his peers circulated. The most destructive was the rumor he hit his ex-girlfriend. Due to misinformation and rumors, many friends turned on him without knowing the truth. People labeled him "the bad guy." He told me in a heart-to-heart conversation that he once pushed her away during an argument so that he could walk past her, but he swore incessantly that he never hit her. I believed him.

However, the damage was done. All of the rumors were destroying him and his confidence. Albert could not accept that others thought of him as this type of a person. I found him crying many times in Steven's room. I kept telling him that everyone would know the truth in the end. I told him that those who lied to make themselves look better would ultimately bring bad karma to themselves.

The night before Steven's eighteenth birthday, Steven worked until ten o'clock. Albert called Steven's cell phone twice that August evening, but Steven was unable to answer it. When Steven's shift ended, he returned Albert's calls, but Albert did not answer. This was typical because he started work the next morning at five o'clock.

The next morning, Steven received a call that changed his life. Albert tried to commit suicide the night before. Albert's mom had left for work, and his siblings were getting ready when his younger brother discovered Albert still in bed. He immediately assumed that Albert overslept and missed work. He approached Albert, who told him to call their mom because he needed help. His brother handed the phone to Albert, who told his mother that he swallowed two bottles of pills. After the phone call, he passed out. His mother sent for an ambulance, and they took Albert to the closest hospital.

Steven was in shock from the news. He and several friends went to the hospital. Steven phoned me a few hours later to tell me that the doctors had stabilized Albert. Steven returned home around four o'clock that afternoon. As a family, we took him out for his birthday dinner in order to help settle his mind and be together.

After dinner, we received an update. Albert's vital signs were diminishing. Because his brain was hemorrhaging, he was flown to the Mayo Hospital. I told Steven that I would drive him and a few of his friends there. They were all devastated and in no condition to drive.

When we arrived, the waiting room was full of people for Albert including high school kids, his pastor, his parents, and his siblings. Many were praying in groups. I guided a group of kids in prayer.

After several hours, many had gone home. I saw Albert's mother sitting by herself with her head in her hands. I had never met her before. I approached her and asked if she believed in healings. She replied, "Yes." Based on the bond she had with her son, I told her that I would work with her to send healing energy to him. I also told her that this energy was from the Highest Divine. I told her I was only the vessel and that my guides told me to place my hands on her head while standing behind her.

Because many kids were watching and I was having trouble concentrating on my guides, I removed myself spiritually from them. I prayed that God would fill him with His white light and that the hemorrhaging would cease in his brain.

While we were performing this healing, Albert was in a CAT scan. His mother continued to worry about his bleeding because she had seen his test results firsthand. Because a friend of hers worked at the prior hospital, she was able to review his results before they transferred him. She also told me that Albert was born with a blood clot in his brain that could burst at anytime. If it burst, he could go into a seizure, or worse, die.

When we finished, we sat and held hands for a long time. What we had experienced together seemed to have brought her peace. Without knowing Albert's outcome, I knew that it was time for me to leave. Steven agreed to stay the night with Albert's mother.

The next morning, Albert's mother called to tell me that the CAT scan showed the hemorrhaging had stopped and the blood clot was gone. Although it appeared that our healing worked and that he survived an unfortunate circumstance, Albert was not out of the woods. He was still comatose. More perplexing, the doctors did not understand why because he was not sedated.

Albert's mother asked me if I would return to the hospital to be with Albert. I replied, "Of course, but how would I get into his intensive care room?" Given his critical status, I needed to be a family member to go in. She said that she would tell them I was from his church. It worked.

When I arrived, Albert's arms were tied at his sides. The doctor said that if he had withdrawals, these bands would help since he had tubes going down his throat and many monitors on. The doctors were watching his kidneys closely because they were worried about failure. As I stood there, I saw his deceased grandmother on the other side of the bed with him. I shared this with his mother. She told me that he was close to his grandmother.

Next, my guides and angels told me specifically what would happen next. I explained to Albert's mother that in fifteen minutes, at 3:15 p.m. specifically, Albert was going to begin vomiting. She needed to get the doctors to remove his tubes or he would gag. The spirits were giving her time to understand what was about to occur. It was clear that Albert needed to rid his body of the toxins. Albert had swallowed one bottle of Ibuprofen and one bottle of Percocet, both pain medications.

In his hospital room, I placed my hands over Albert's stomach area and moved them wherever the angels guided me. At exactly 3:15 p.m., Albert started vomiting exactly how we anticipated. Even though his mother was prepared, it was understandably difficult for her to watch Albert in such a state. His doctors and nurses ran into the room and immediately removed all of his tubes. Although I did not want to, I asked them if I should leave. A doctor turned to me and told me emphatically to stay. He said, "You are the only one who seems to understand what is going on..." His reaction to my question totally astonished me.

After Albert's system was cleansed, Albert woke up. He and his mother reunited. She was elated and grateful. Through the work of my guides, angels, and the Highest Divine, I was used as a communication vessel from above. We believe that a true miracle was performed. I continue to be amazed. Not only did I witness this miracle firsthand, I was given the privilege to guide that day's events.

Because of Albert's belief in my healing ability and his overall trust in me, I believe that his spirit allowed this healing to take place. Fortunately, Albert walked away from this experience without any serious complications. This was an enormous lesson for my entire family, as well as for Albert's. We learned that life is precious and that one should be grateful for each day.

I often wonder what would have happened if the outcome was different.

At the time, both my son and Albert were about to start college. Before and during the healing, I felt strongly that this healing would have the outcome I wanted for both Albert and for my son. They both needed to continue their path in life.

Today, both boys are attending college and working. With help, Albert resumed his normal life. He is content and appreciative for each day. I thank my angels, guides, and the Highest Divine for this wonderful gift. In my eyes, it was a perfect healing.

CHARLIE

The next healing occurred in March 2004. I received a call from a family that I had never met before. They were told about me through mutual friends. Because their son was in a coma, they asked for my help. For purposes of this book, I will call him Charlie.

Simply put, Charlie was in the wrong place at the wrong time. He was with a friend, and together they were asked if they wanted to go for a ride with another boy. Although Charlie did not know him well, his friend did, so they agreed. Soon thereafter, the driver said that he needed to make a stop. The stop was to pick up cocaine.

Everything was fine until Charlie heard sirens. Because the driver was speeding, a police car was in pursuit. Charlie panicked because the cocaine was also in the car. He knew that he did not want to be caught with it—what would happen to him? For one, he knew that he would be in big trouble with his parents. Charlie therefore quickly swallowed eight balls of cocaine. Fortunately, or unfortunately, the police officer only gave the driver a ticket.

Next, rather than taking Charlie to a hospital to pump his stomach, the three boys concluded that the cocaine bags would pass through him and he would be fine. After one hour, Charlie's body started into convulsions. The plastic bags were dissolving, thereby dumping all of the cocaine into Charlie's system. The driver ran from the situation because he did not want any part of it. Charlie's friend called 911 and rushed him to emergency.

By the time I was called, Charlie was in a coma. The doctors had also asked his parents if they wanted to pull the ventilator. On my way to the hospital, I again asked my guides, angels, and the Highest Divine to assist me with Charlie.

Charlie's mother greeted me outside of the intensive care unit. We had never met before. I explained to them that I am not a healer *per se* and that they should not expect a miracle from me. I told them that I am only a messenger and that Charlie's outcome was ultimately up to Charlie and the Highest Divine. They understood.

When I saw Charlie, I realized that he was the same age as my oldest son. He was only seventeen. I thought to myself that this could be my son lying there. I held Charlie's hand and told him who I was. I told him that I could hear him. Through me, Charlie began sharing special moments of his childhood with his parents. He said things that convinced his parents it was their son talking and not me.

Charlie then explained to his parents that he was with the Highest Divine. God told him that He would share with Charlie what his life would be like if he were to live. Next, Charlie told his parents to trust him and his decision. If he thought it was better to leave this world, it would be for the best.

Charlie's mother asked what she should do next. She did not want to make the decision to pull the plug on the ventilator. Charlie told his parents that he would have something in his body shut down so it would be obvious that it was his decision to leave this world. Then no one would have to make the difficult choice to pull the ventilator.

Our session with Charlie ended there. The family needed to wait and see what would happen next. I found it truly amazing how this entire family had so much trust in me given we had just met moments before.

When I was leaving, Charlie's mother asked if I would go with her to the hospital chapel. Because there were many high school friends in the hallways, we guided them to the chapel with us. She held my hand tightly while she introduced me. I was unsure what to say to them, but I believe the spirits helped me lead a prayer. I then asked that the kids go home so that Charlie's parents could have time with their son. It was not doing anyone any good just waiting in the hallways.

I also reassured them that Charlie could hear their prayers. I encouraged them to continue to pray. If they wanted to write a letter to Charlie, they could. I knew this would be an excellent exercise for them because they could release any guilt or pain they were experiencing. Such writing can be a very healing process given the overwhelming emotion associated with such a tragedy. His mother agreed to leave a basket outside of her home. If they wanted the letter to be read to Charlie, I asked that it be unsealed. If they only wanted Charlie to receive it, then I instructed them to seal the letter in an envelope.

My time at the hospital was finished. Charlie's mother and I embraced hoping for the best, and not knowing what was meant to be.

Nearly twenty-four hours later, I received a call from Charlie's family. Charlie's heart had failed. He chose to cross over. I had a knot in my stomach and began to cry. I felt the pain for this family. According to the doctors, Charlie's heart had been fine. This must have been what he was referring to because he told us that he would make it very clear if he decided not to return. There was nothing that could have saved him.

That same evening I spoke with Charlie's father to give him my blessings.

He told me that what happened in our meeting came to fruition and that he was grateful. He said that he was at peace with his son's decision to pass over—as strange as that may sound coming from a father experiencing life's greatest tragedy, the loss of a child.

The outcome was not what I wanted, but it also was not in my hands. I was the vessel that Charlie used to talk with his parents. The purpose of this healing was not to "heal" Charlie, but to bring peace to his parents given the outcome of this tragic situation.

I also learned so much from Charlie and our time together. I have since shared with many how people in comas can hear and wish they could communicate back to their loved ones. To Charlie, I say thank you for trusting in someone you just met. By trusting in me and using me as the messenger, Charlie brought peace to his family, friends, and loved ones.

Six months later, my son Steven was at a party. The kids were reminiscing about Charlie. They spoke of a woman who helped him communicate with his family while comatose. It did not occur to Steven initially that I was the woman they were describing. Once he made the connection, he shared with them that this woman was his mom. They told Steven that what I did for this family was truly amazing. The family's peace with Charlie's passing was unbelievable. I was grateful to know the little I did that day continued to touch so many.

BETTY

The next healing occurred in September 2004. I was reading emails when I received a message from my in-laws. One of their friend's daughters was diagnosed with cancer of the mouth. For this book, I will call her Betty. Betty had been through significant treatments over the prior few years with hospital time, feeding tubes, etc.

Betty was a wife and a young mother of two. My in-laws were asking me for prayers for her. Given this, I placed Betty on a prayer list. I requested prayers of healing to rid her mouth of the cancer.

Without knowing it, the day I placed her on the prayer list was the same day she was at Stanford Hospital in California to discuss her history, scans, biopsy, and next course of treatment. The doctors suggested to Betty that she do surgery and then follow with four weeks of radiation and chemotherapy. She left the hospital discouraged and drained, but ready for the next endeavor.

I had never met Betty, but her parents knew of me through my in-laws. They asked them if they thought there was anything I could do. They had no idea that I had already placed Betty on a prayer list. The next day, after only one day of prayers, the head doctor called Betty back. He told her that he was studying her reports again and that there may be a false reading. Some of the test results were not making sense to him.

After further review, he cancelled all of her appointments, including the surgery, and asked to see her in six weeks for a follow-up check. Apparently, she had a cold and sinus infection that skewed her test results. Even so, Betty's cancer appeared to be cured. The new tests did not show any cancer whatsoever. Her loved ones were all shocked, elated, and relieved.

I then received an email from Betty's family, which read, "Whatever Debbie may have done, she may have done a lot. Wow. We are amazed." I too was amazed. This was a clear blessing to watch. All of the events took place on the same day without us ever knowing. The story validated the power of prayer and the strength of the healing energy sent through it. I must thank everyone who prayed for Betty. It is over one year and Betty is still cancer-free.

JAN

Finally, my last example of a healing occurred in November 2004. My best friend Jan was diagnosed with lung cancer. There were two spots on her lungs that had grown measurably compared to the prior year. Consequently, the doctors said they needed to remove the spots.

When I heard the news, I was devastated. Jan was the closest friend I had here on earth. She knew me better than anyone did. She was in the room when I gave birth to my fourth child. We even considered ourselves sisters. I thought to myself, "Why Jan? This cannot be happening to her."

Because Jan is as spiritual, or even more spiritual, than myself, she recognized that she had choices to make. She knew she could choose to fight the cancer, or she could just let it take over. We discussed this in great length. Jan said, "Well, for my children, I should fight and stay. Although life can be so hard at times…"

When I heard her say this, I realized that someone from the other side was trying to talk through me. They were very angry. It was her grandparents who had passed on. They said, "Now Jan, stop this. You need to fight this for *your* will to live, not the will to live for your children. It won't work if it is not for you."

I relayed this message. It was heavy and powerful. I was an emotional mess. After her grandparents, I knew that it was my turn to yell at her. I told her that she had better put up a good fight because I was not ready to lose her either!

A few days after these discussions, Jan agreed to have a healing performed on her. Jan and I knew a couple that were both Reiki masters. Reiki is defined as a spiritually guided healing energy that is directed by the

Highest Divine. The word Reiki (ray-key) is made from two Japanese words. The first, "rei," means Wisdom of God. The second, "ki," means vital life force. Once a person becomes a Reiki Master and wishes to do a healing, they place their hands on or near an area of the body. Reiki can treat the whole person, including the body, emotions, mind, and spirit.

The couple agreed to perform the healing in hopes of eliminating the cancer. They also agreed to allow me to assist them. Jan rested on a massage table with her eyes closed. The couple stood on each side of her, and I was at her feet. During the healing, Jan saw a medicine man on a horse enter the room. We knew the healing was finished when Jan told us that the medicine man disappeared.

After we were finished, Jan told us that she felt like her body was uncontrollably shaking during the healing process. We reassured her that she had been lying perfectly still. We all were unsure about what had just occurred. All we could do was trust in the healing, pray, and wait.

The following week, Jan went in for surgery to remove the two spots. She knew they would take the spots out and possibly some of her lung. When the surgery was complete, the doctors said that they did not find cancer, but valley fever. Valley fever is a fungus infection that typically affects the lungs. The fungus lives in soil but is spread through the air. It is an illness that is often deceptive to doctors because it has symptoms similar to other illnesses. It typically affects people where there is movement of dirt, for example, through construction or earthquakes. It is often found in the southwestern United States.

Like many of the people who have valley fever, Jan had no signs of it. They removed what they called valley fever spots, making Jan cancer-free. It was amazing news and an enormous relief for us all. Because they removed part of her lung, her recovery was painful. Even so, it made Jan truly value life and all that she had to live for.

I am grateful that Jan chose to have the will to live for herself and listen to her grandparents. I am grateful to our friends for performing such an amazing healing and allowing me to participate in it. I knew I could not have done this with out them. Jan was too close of a friend to take this on alone.

I am grateful to the universe for giving me more time with my best friend. Jan continues to live cancer-free. However, I am sad that she will be leaving Arizona because its hot weather makes it too hard for her to breathe. I know wherever she moves, as long as she is happy and follows her heart, that I will be at peace. I can only hope that we will continue to walk through life together despite our distance.

I also learned a very special lesson through this experience. Jan's grandparents said it best. If you have a will to live for yourself, you can beat anything! Miracles are often attained through healings. Again, I do not consider myself a healer. In fact, it is not often that I am called for a healing. When I am, I know I can only do it with the support of my angels, guides, and Highest Divine. I must trust that no matter the reason for my calling, I am needed. I must also remember that I am only the vessel. The healing comes only from the Highest Divine.

✦ 4 ✦

Spirit Guides

ON THE EVENING OF JUNE 24, 2003, I performed a reading for a gentleman named Don that had lost both of his parents as well as his two brothers. He was the only surviving member from his immediate family. It was a challenging reading because he wanted so badly to have validation from each of his deceased family members. He wanted to know for sure I connected with the right spirits and if they were all content. It also proved to be a powerful reading because this reading not only brought peace to him, but it brought about a life-changing event for me as a medium.

Because Don was a spiritual man, one of his co-workers, who was also a friend of mine, referred him to me for a reading. Prior to our meeting, Don had actively studied and researched various theories about the afterlife. Consequently, Don was anxious and ready to receive information from his loved ones who had passed.

At the time of our reading, I was still learning to trust my spirit guides and lacked the confidence to say out loud what I was hearing, particularly names of those who had passed over. Even so, Don told me at the end of our reading that he was extremely pleased. The messages that came through were numerous, specific, and in many cases, known only to Don and his deceased loved ones. Don told me that he thought I would soon confidently speak the names of the spirits talking. He asked that when this happened for me, that I call him back for another reading.

When I was leaving, a book fell off the coffee table and landed on his foot. Don, nor I, bumped the table. It was as if the book jumped off the table by itself. We both stopped and stared. Don picked it up and handed it to me. He asked me if I had ever read the book. I had not. The title of the book was *The Afterlife Experiments* by Dr. Gary E. Schwartz.[4] Don encouraged me to read the book and loaned me his copy.

Looking back, Don and I both believe that the events of our meeting were not a coincidence, notably, why, how and when this book fell to the floor. It was a clear sign for me to read the book, which I completed days later. I was enthralled and could not put it down. In the back of the book listed other books Dr. Schwartz recommended on similar topics. One, in particular, was called *The Afterlife Codes* by Susy Smith.[5] For whatever reason, this book stood out on the list, and I was compelled to read it next.

When I finished it, I felt as though I had a message for Susy Smith, the book's author. That is, while reading the book, an unknown spirit contacted me and told me how a medium could break these so-called "afterlife codes" that she wrote about in her book. The spirit persistently contacted me with a sense of urgency and wanted me to get this message to Susy Smith as soon as possible. For whatever reason, I felt as though I needed to oblige this spirit.

Her book indicated that she resided in Tucson, Arizona. I then recalled that in Dr. Schwartz's book, it stated he worked at the University of Arizona at the Human Energy Lab, in Tucson, Arizona. When I flipped back through *The Afterlife Codes*, I then read that Susy Smith "adopted" Dr. Schwartz, making her his "adopted" grandmother. Although the adoption was not official, they adored and respected one another and developed a strong working relationship as well as friendship. Based on this fact, I knew in order to get a message to Susy Smith, it may be easiest to go through Dr. Schwartz at the university.

Ironically, my oldest son attended the University of Arizona; therefore, I had easy access to all of the campus phone numbers. All I needed to do was convince Dr. Schwartz that I legitimately had a message for Susy Smith and hope that he would help me.

When I placed the call to Dr. Schwartz's office, I reached his answering machine. Fortunately, his greeting included his email address as well. I left a message for him on his machine summarizing my reason for contacting him. I then followed up with a detailed email.

In the email, I explained to him that I was a medium who resided in Phoenix, Arizona. I told him that I had an important message for Susy Smith and inquired if he could help me contact her. I also stated that I would be interested in volunteering at the Human Energy Lab.

With further research, I later learned that Dr. Schwartz was the head of this lab (the VERITAS Research Program),[6] and its ultimate mission was to prove that a medium, such as myself, could contact the spirit world. Through research and experiments, Dr. Schwartz and his colleagues' main objective was to focus on facts, not feelings.

More specifically, I read that Dr. Schwartz stated that he is not trying to prove the existence of survival of consciousness. To the contrary, what he is trying to do is give survival of consciousness, if it exists, the opportunity to prove itself. Based on this, I figured if I volunteered my time at the lab, I not only could help them with their research, but I would better my chances of meeting Susy Smith.

Several weeks passed before I received a response to my email. Dr. Julie Beischel sent me an email from the lab. She told me that she worked with Dr. Schwartz. I later learned that she was considered his right-hand researcher. She stated that she was interested in meeting me. Because our meeting did not occur right away due to scheduling conflicts, I was pushed by this unknown spirit to remain in contact with her on a consistent basis. As a result, we emailed regularly, both learning about one another and the lab.

Dr. Beischel asked if I would be interested in a double-blind experiment in my home. I agreed. Double-blind meant that I would not be given the spirit's identity. In addition, Dr. Beischel would be a proxy-sitter, meaning she would sit in for a designated person wanting a reading from this unknown spirit. This way, if I was also psychic, I could not read the sitter's mind. I would only relay the information I received from the spirit pertinent to its loved one. From a research perspective, this was the ideal way to test my skills in contacting the spirit world.

It took eight months from the time I completed my reading with Don to this meeting with Dr. Beischel. I was excited to have a chance to share my story with her because I firmly believed there were no coincidences. The purpose of our meeting started when Dr. Schwartz's book fell on Don's foot, which compelled me to read Susy Smith's book, and then ended with my need to deliver a message to Susy Smith. I could not emphasize enough to Dr. Beischel how pushy this spirit was in prodding me to contact her.

When I finished sharing my story with Dr. Beischel, she sat there staring at me. She was smiling, but I did not know why. Apparently, my story came as no surprise to her. Dr. Beischel explained to me that Susy Smith was the Founder of the Human Energy Lab. She also told me that Susy Smith passed away five years prior. She said that Susy Smith told Dr. Schwartz that when she crossed over into the afterlife, she would send mediums to him and guide them to say that they had a message from her. It was amazing to hear that her work at the Human Energy Lab here on earth continued into the next life. I was absolutely flabbergasted. I had finally learned that the unknown spirit who had contacted me and pushed me for months was Susy Smith herself!

Susy Smith was the one who made the book fall! She guided me to read the two books! She encouraged me to contact the lab! This is why I felt such a drive to follow through and not give up! To this day, I am amazed by the fact that spirits can guide me without my acknowledging that it is them pushing me to complete a task.

I will be forever grateful to Susy Smith for being my guide to Dr. Schwartz and Dr. Beischel. I know now Susy Smith put me in touch with Dr. Schwartz so that I could help him continue to prove that an afterlife truly exists.

I will never forget my first reading with Dr. Beischel. According to Dr. Beischel, I did very well on the reading I did that day. However, I unfortunately cannot comment further on the reading because it is part of their research for the lab. I am not told the particulars of what I get right and wrong. Rather, they only give me a general impression. Overall, they said that they have been "pleased with my results." Therefore, their research with me continues.

✦   ✦   ✦

In June 2004, Dr. Beischel and I drove to Tucson, Arizona together. It was the first time I would have the opportunity to meet Dr. Schwartz in person. They wanted me to participate in an experiment with Dr. Schwartz and his producers at the Human Energy Lab. Together, they were all working on a documentation of mediums.

For the meeting, they asked me to do a phone reading in Dr. Schwartz's office. Dr. Beischel sat next to me on my left, Dr. Schwartz sat across from me, and his producers video and audio taped me from the back of the room.

Again, I was not given the deceased name or the sitter's name during this reading. Both Dr. Schwartz and Dr. Beischel were extremely pleased with the reading results, although they did not disclose details to me. However, they approved my including one part of the reading for this book.

During the reading, the unknown spirit told me that there was a little dog with him. The sitter told me I was mistaken because he never had a dog. Even so, I felt strongly about the presence of the dog with him and kept firm that this spirit was showing me a dog next to him.

The dog proved to be invaluable information to Dr. Schwartz. Prior to my meeting with them, Dr. Schwartz asked the spirit, who he had known well in life, to show me this dog in order to prove that I was not a fraud. Dr. Schwartz told me later that it was nice to see that I trusted what I was hearing and seeing and was not persuaded by another's reactions. Ironically, the sitter stated repeatedly that I was very much incorrect, yet it turned out that I was very much right.

Once again, I must say thank you to the spirits. They allowed me to show my abilities when it counted most. I also say thank you to Dr. Schwartz and Dr. Beischel for their kindness. They make my job easy. With their support, compassion, and trust in the afterlife, I have since gained the confidence to receive and trust in the words I receive from spirits. I am no longer afraid to share the names that I am hearing.

I have also learned that the information I receive during a reading may not make sense to a sitter at first, but it may come true when the time is right for them to receive the message. This has happened on a fairly consistent basis, where the sitters follow up and tell me about something that was unaccounted for in a reading thereafter comes to pass and makes perfect sense.

As stated before, I believe that spirits walk with me daily. Sometimes I do not know who these spirits are, but always trust that they are guiding me for the right reason. The spirit of Susy Smith may have pushed me, but I ultimately had to make a choice to continue with her mission. When a person asks a spirit what direction they should go in life, they need to understand that we have free will to do what we desire. The spirits cannot tell us what to do; they can only guide and encourage us.

If you feel that your direction in life is constantly coming to a dead end and is a complete struggle, then perhaps the spirits are trying to help you see that you need change. If life is flowing easily, then staying the course may be appropriate for you. One must trust that what happens in one's life is all happening for a reason. We may never understand these reasons while on earth, but these uncertainties may be clear once we cross over. May you enjoy your journey through life knowing you are never alone.

✦   ✦   ✦

<u>Susy Smith</u>

(1911 to 2001)
"It is too coincidental to be accidental."

✦5✦

<u>Dying</u>

LETTING GO OF A LOVED ONE may be the hardest challenge one faces while on this earth. We all deal with death differently and grieve in our own unique way. For some, death may be a celebration of a loved one's life; for others, it may mean considerable mourning and emptiness. Of course, it may also be a combination of both. There is no right or wrong way to view death.

One may wonder what would happen without particular loved ones in his or her life. It is the simple things–their touch, their smell, their laughter, or their conversation–that we typically miss, making death hard to accept and carry on. More often than not, people view death as a loss rather than a new beginning for our loved one who passed on. If people embraced the notion of a new beginning, then facing death would likely be a lot less scary and empty.

The purpose of this chapter is to confirm that life truly does continue in the afterlife. I witnessed this through a dying friend. In June 2005, I completed a phone reading for a man named Dick Mitchell, although his friends called him "Mitch." The parents of my son's friend, Luke, referred him to me.

Prior to the reading, I learned that Mitch had contacted several psychics, but none was truly reputable. Even so, he received format letters from them once a month, as long as his credit card was available to charge. In my opinion, it is a dreadful shame that these so-called psychics take advantage of people like this. Because Mitch had terminal brain cancer, he was grasping at whatever he could find that would give him a glimpse of hope into the afterlife. He wanted to know that it did exist. His doctors were uncertain how long he had here on earth, and he questioned what was going to happen to him when he passed on.

In our first phone meeting, his parents and his grandmother came through from the spirit world. Mitch's grandmother told him that when he met his new granddaughter that he would see a special sparkle in her eye. She told him that after he met her, he would then view life differently. Mitch validated that his daughter had just delivered a baby girl and that he had not yet seen the baby. He was anxious to meet her as soon as possible.

After our formal reading, we discussed how people deal with others that are facing death. Mitch told me that it was incredibly upsetting to know that you must leave your friends and family, but it was more painful to learn who your real friends were during the dying process.

I tried to help him understand that many people do not know how to cope with someone who is dying. Most would rather run from it out of fear rather than face the unknown. Seeing a good friend grow weaker and pass away was hard to witness. Even though some of his friends may have withdrawn normal contact, I told him that I believed deep down they still loved him. I told him that their lack of contact was their way of coping with the fact that he would not be here for them much longer. Although this response was ironic—running from a person when he needed it most—it was not uncommon.

We ended our conversation and planned to speak again, but next time in person. Until then, I told Mitch to journal his feelings. I also stressed to him to take the opportunity and say all of the words that needed to be said to everyone he cared about and loved.

✦　✦　✦

Mitch contacted me about one week later to set up our next meeting. Given his weakening state, he was living between houses with dear friends. I would have volunteered my home for the reading, but with four children out of school for the summer, there were no quiet spots. As such, Mitch suggested Luke's house. They had referred him to me, and he was quite comfortable in their home. This was also a convenient meeting place because they suggested I bring my youngest two children along. This way, I did not have to watch the clock and could stay as long as necessary.

When my children and I arrived, Luke's mother Karen greeted us. The children all went to the back of the house, and Karen brought me to meet Mitch. Mitch was standing in the hall. He had been waiting for me to arrive.

My first impression of Mitch was that he was a kind man. He had incredible blue eyes that felt as though he could look through you. I later told Karen that I thought he looked like Paul Newman. She laughed because I was not the first to think this. She said that when he was younger, girls would remark on his resemblance to Paul Newman. Mitch would tell them that he was Paul Newman's brother, and they believed it!

Karen, Mitch, and I sat in the family room to conduct our second reading. Before we started, Mitch mentioned that he was concerned about making a final trip to Minnesota. Mitch had two daughters who lived there, one of which had just given birth to the baby girl his grandmother referenced in our first reading. Mitch stated that the most important thing he did before he died was meet his new granddaughter. He was anxious to look into her eyes and see "the sparkle."

Mitch asked me if I thought that he was capable of driving from Arizona to Minnesota. Karen voiced her concern that the cancer in Mitch's brain had worsened. She worried he could blackout while driving and hurt someone, or himself. Karen and I agreed that it was no longer safe for him to drive to Minnesota, but flying was an option.

Flying to Minnesota was unacceptable to Mitch. He was a man that did not want to burden anyone. If he flew, then he would have no car and would have to rely on others to drive him once he arrived. Mitch agreed to think this idea through more.

We then posed another question to Mitch. What would happen if he traveled to Minnesota, became worse, and therefore was unable to return to Arizona? Did he know where he wanted to die? Mitch was the type of person who did not want to impose on anyone. He told us that he wanted to rent a hotel room where he could die. He did not care if it was in Minnesota or Arizona, to him it did not matter. He was totally serious.

His perspective did not go over well with either Karen or me. Karen tried to make him understand that he would not be burdening her if he wanted to die in her home. In fact, she told him that she would be honored if he chose to do so. I then told him that I do not believe anyone should ever die alone if he or she had the choice. Mitch conceded and to re-think where he would reside when the time came for his passing. Karen and I together acknowledged it was a fair compromise.

We then proceeded with the reading. Mitch's first question was "Who will be there for me when I cross over?" I told him that his grandmother said that she would be there for him. Mitch replied, "Why my grandmother?" The only thing that he remembered about her from his childhood was that she was mean. I then saw his grandmother smile. She said to me, "No, I was not mean, I was stern." I relayed the message and told him that he would learn that she was nice and that she meant well when he was a child.

Mitch seemed very unsettled with the idea of his mean grandmother greeting him. He said that he needed someone else there he could trust in order to make it easier for him to cross over. Everyone was silent for a moment, including the spirits. Then my father, who had never come through to me in another person's reading, showed himself. He came through to tell Mitch that he too would be there for him.

I told Mitch that my father's name was Frank and that he had passed away. My father continued speaking through me. He said, "I will be there for you. Because you have so much trust in Debbie, you will therefore have trust in me." Mitch said that he would like that. The spirits gave Mitch what he needed to hear that day, and we ended the reading.

Next, the three of us looked at one another with a great sense of peace. Mitch and I were sitting on the same couch facing a window that looked outside. Karen was sitting on the couch next to ours, with her back to the window. While we continued conversing, I saw something go by the window outside. Although I knew it was a spirit, I looked at Mitch and asked him if he saw it too. He said yes and agreed that he thought that it was a spirit. We both saw the same figurine shadow. Its density was not like ours, and we both saw no face with it.

With all of the excitement, Karen was astonished and could not believe what she heard. She wanted to check things out for herself. Karen thought that perhaps it was someone coming over for one of her kids. She looked out of the window, yet saw nothing. She then went outside and looked around, but she still found nothing. To this day, I do not know if she believes that it was a spirit, but for Mitch and me, there is no question that it was a spirit.

Seeing a spirit brought up even more concerns for Mitch. Mitch wanted to know if I would be able to see, smell, or hear him once he crossed over. He questioned, "What will I be able to do from the other side?" I told him that I am able to hear the spirits voices extremely well and often they reveal themselves to me.

I then told him what I knew: Spirits send signs to their loved ones to let them know that they are around. Spirits make themselves known in various ways. Just thinking about a loved one who passed may lead a spirit to touch you. You can literally feel its gentle touch, or the spirit may surround you with a sense of coolness or warmth. The spirit may choose to send a bird, a butterfly, or anything else that it believes is appropriate to represent itself to a loved one. The spirit may unexpectedly send a familiar smell or aroma to arouse treasured memories. Spirits can also move things around. You may find a book or picture that seemed to fall out of nowhere. Often with such a sight, a smell, or a presence, calmness may overcome you. It is the spirit trying to get your attention.

I then asked, "Mitch, what is it that you would like to do for us so that we will know that it is you coming through?" Mitch replied. "You will know it's me by the scent of cabbage rolls." This was something Karen and Mitch made together. We all agreed that this would be a strong smell and no one would miss it. We all laughed. The spirit we saw that night gave Mitch a glimpse of hope that he too would one day be a spirit sending messages to his loved ones.

Mitch had one more question before I left. He asked, "Is it okay if I called you by a nickname?" I said, "Sure, you can call me anything you wish." Mitch explained that I reminded him of a good friend from his high school days. He called her "Red." He said, "Can I call you Red?"

I said okay, but I told him that he did not have any idea what this name meant to me. I then explained.

Because I did not have red hair–I was blond–his calling me "Red" was no coincidence. I had tears in my eyes when I told Mitch that my father was nicknamed "Red" all of his life. All of our family and friends called him "Red." Since my father came through during our reading saying that he would be there for Mitch, and then Mitch had this compulsion to call me "Red," confirmed to me that this reading was very powerful for the both of us. I told that him our paths had crossed for a reason. I told Mitch since my father would be in the afterlife waiting for him to pass that I would be honored to help him from this side. Mitch agreed and felt relieved, satisfied, and tired. We called it a night. As we hugged goodbye, we committed to keeping in close contact with one another.

✛ ✛ ✛

After exactly one week and no contact, I drove into Karen's driveway to take one of my son's to her home. While in my car, I saw Mitch in the distance. He seemed distraught. He was pacing looking in the grass as if he lost something. He did not recognize me in the car. After watching him for a bit, I was uncertain what to do. Since I had my young daughter in the backseat, I decided to leave to prevent him from being embarrassed or uncomfortable.

The next day, because I was still upset about watching Mitch and his actions, I called Karen at her work to check in. She confirmed for me what I had thought. Mitch was becoming disorientated and was deteriorating quickly. Karen told me that she was worried about him. I told her that I would give him a call.

During my phone conversation with Mitch, he told me that he was experiencing severe head pain. He was failing quickly. I encouraged him to contact hospice. I told him that they could administer medication to help keep him comfortable. He agreed to contact them as soon as we hung up.

From this phone call forward, everything seemed to happen incredibly fast. The next events took place within five days. I am grateful to my family and to Mitch's family for allowing me to spend the amount of time I needed to with Mitch.

The following morning I received a phone call from Karen that Mitch was about to be transported by ambulance to Scottsdale Memorial Hospital. He was experiencing an unbearable pain in his head. Karen followed the ambulance to ensure that he received proper treatment. Karen knew him well enough to be his voice, as well as his eyes and ears.

After four hours, she called and told me that he was resting peacefully. Later that day, I joined Karen at the hospital with her husband Dale and their good friend Harvey. I felt as though it was a great honor to be invited because they had all been close friends for over twenty years.

A nurse was in the room when we arrived. We all stood at the foot of Mitch's bed as the nurse put down his dinner tray. Mitch looked up. The first words he said to us were, "Red, Red is here!" I smiled. The nurse replied, "Well, you know her, but can you tell me the names of everyone else?" Mitch was slow, but was able to say everyone else's name correctly. The nurse was testing Mitch's mental abilities because of his rapid deterioration from the brain cancer.

We told the nurse that we would help Mitch with his dinner. I noticed that he was having difficulty swallowing. Karen told me that the cancer had spread to his lungs causing it to be painful for him to swallow. She also said that the cancer had now spread throughout his body and into many of his organs. Although Mitch seemed comfortable on the outside, Karen knew his prognosis was grim.

That night we stayed late, past the hospital closing hours. On our way home, Karen, Dale, and Harvey shared many memories about Mitch. Through the stories, I learned a lot about him and what an enormous impact he had on others. He was a good man, an honorable man.

When we arrived at Karen and Dale's home, Dale walked me to my car. He brought up the fact that Mitch's first word that night was "Red." Dale witnessed for the first time the spiritual relationship Mitch and I developed. He also shared with me that Mitch told him he felt a real connection with me. I told him that I never knew it was possible to love someone so much after only knowing him for a few weeks. He thanked me for coming and for being there for Mitch.

On my drive home, an odd feeling overcame me. I knew that I was losing a dear friend, but I also felt as if I was losing my father again. I cried the entire way home.

✝　✝　✝

The next day, when I went to visit Mitch, Dale was standing outside of his hospital room. By the look on his face, I knew Mitch was not doing well. Dale was visibly upset over watching his dear friend struggle. We embraced without any spoken words. I proceeded into Mitch's room.

Karen was beside Mitch, holding his hand. Mitch's wrists were tied to the hospital bed rails because Mitch had tried to leave the hospital several times. During the night, Mitch did not understand where he was or why he had to be there, so he tried to escape.

When I saw him, he was somewhat coherent, but he was experiencing severe cold sweats. He also struggled to speak. We agreed to only ask him "yes" or "no" questions to ease this burden. He squeezed our hand to answer "yes."

As the two of us sat by his bedside wiping his forehead with a cool cloth, Mitch looked into our eyes and struggled to say his last words. He said, "They are here." I asked, "Who? Mitch, tell me who!" After sheer exhaustion and determination, he replied "Frank." This was the last word Mitch spoke.

I was incredibly relieved to know that my father was in the room with us all. When he said, "They are here," I was assuming that he was referring to my father and his grandmother who came through in our reading. I had tears of joy in my eyes. My father was following through with his commitment to Mitch. He was there for Mitch, but his presence held significance for me.

This was such an incredible gift. Mitch reinforced the notion that what I hear from the spiritual world in a reading are true words. Again, I only relay messages, but to see such follow-through exemplifies true love and compassion from my father and his grandmother. I was elated and comforted knowing my father was close by.

I knew that it would not be long before Mitch would pass given the presence of these spirits. Karen called Mitch's daughters to update them on their father's condition and asked that they fly to Arizona to say their final goodbyes. She also contacted Mitch's power of attorney and asked for permission to transfer Mitch to hospice.

The following day, on a Sunday, Mitch was moved to hospice. Although I wanted to visit him again, I knew that I needed to spend time with my family. Karen said she would keep me posted. She later called to say he was settled and stable.

On Monday morning, I went with Karen to hospice. Because I had never experienced hospice before, I did not know what to expect. I was pleasantly surprised when I saw Mitch. He had been recently shaven and cleaned. His hands were no longer tied to the bed rails. His bed tilted upward, and he was breathing much slower. Hospice had administered medication to help Mitch rest comfortably. He looked as though he was at peace.

The hospice setting was very different from the hospital. I was relieved because I knew that Mitch was in the appropriate care to begin his dying process. Even though Mitch was unable to respond to us, I wondered if he was seeing me when his eyes were looking at me. Karen and I believed that he could hear us and knew we were in the room. Karen told Mitch that because his daughters were arriving the following day, he needed to hang on.

After a few hours with Mitch, we said our goodbyes. For me, I felt like it was my final goodbye with him. I did not know if I would ever see Mitch again.

At seven o'clock Tuesday morning, I woke up and heard a spirit's voice. The voice kept saying, "Cinnamon! Cinnamon!" I wondered who this spirit was. Then Mitch came immediately into my mind. Was this the voice of Mitch? He would certainly be the one to tell me the type of spice I should use because he loved to cook. Then I had the sudden sensation to smile. I knew then that I was correct. It was Mitch. Had he crossed over? Why am I hearing from him now?

I ran down the hallway from my bedroom to the kitchen to call Karen. On the floor in the hallway, I picked up a small piece of paper. It had all of Karen's phone numbers on it. How did it get there in the middle of the night? It was the paper I carried in my purse. Was Mitch messing with me already? To appease Mitch, I told him that I would call Karen right away.

I was interrupted before I could make the phone call. My three-year-old daughter woke up and came into the kitchen saying, "Mommy, I want cinnamon." I could not believe what I heard her say. My daughter is predictable when it comes to breakfast. I sit her down at our kitchen table, place a bowl of cereal in front of her, and let her watch cartoons. However, that day, of all days, she requested cinnamon. She does not even know what cinnamon is! Without debate, I made her cinnamon toast, thanks to Mitch. I now had confirmation that this spirit was Mitch. Again, there were no coincidences.

While my daughter ate her cinnamon toast, I emailed Karen at work. I was writing an email inquiring about Mitch and highlighting the cinnamon story when my phone rang. I was not finished with my email but knew it was Karen before I answered. Karen was on her cell phone on her way to work. She had just received a call from Mitch's daughter saying Mitch should pass at any time. His lungs were filling with fluid. He had been struggling since three o'clock that morning. The dying process for him was nearing the end.

It was convenient for Karen to receive this call on her way to work, because her work happened to be located just past the hospice center. Mitch had once again planned his timing well by not putting Karen out of her way. A man that never wanted to inconvenience anyone continues to live by that credo in his dying moments. I continued to tell Karen about the events that took place before she called. Karen was in awe of the cinnamon story.

I also told her that that Mitch was continuing to teach me lessons in his dying state. That is, I learned that even though Mitch had not yet passed, he was able to leave his body and communicate with me. What a lesson I learned about someone in the dying process!

Karen then said his family was all with him. She told me that she planned to visit Mitch and she would call after he passed. Deep down

I wanted to go, but I felt this was not about me. It was time for Mitch to be with his two girls. The appropriate thing to do was to wait and hear from Karen. As such, I did not ask her if I should go too.

When I hung up, I fell to pieces. I no longer wanted Mitch to die. I felt that I was not ready to let him to go. I did not get to know this man long enough or well enough. In just a matter of weeks, I came to adore him. I went to my bedroom and continued to cry. After such an emotional cry, I was exhausted and rested.

When I checked my clock, it was two o'clock in the afternoon, and I had not heard anything. I needed to take two of my children to a routine doctor's appointment. On my way there, I called Karen's cell phone to leave her a voicemail. I was shocked when Karen answered her phone. I immediately asked if Mitch was all right. Karen replied that he was still hanging on and everyone was there. I asked, "Who was everyone? Can I come?" She replied, "Yes, of course!"

I called my husband in a panic and explained to him that I was going to drop the girls off at the doctor's office. I then planned to head straight for the hospice center. I asked that he take over meeting the girls at the doctor's office. Luckily, he was readily available and could leave work without conflict.

It took me twenty minutes to get to the doctor's office. After I dropped the girls off, the hospice center was only two miles away. So far, everything worked out easily. I would not have been surprised if Mitch was able to control what was going on. I never drove so fast, and fortunately, a police officer did not see me either. All day I prayed to Mitch and repeatedly gave him permission to pass on, but now I was telling him to hang on. I kept praying, "Please hang on until I get there!"

As I entered hospice, I prayed I was not too late. I entered Mitch's room and was relieved to see that he was still alive. He was struggling hard to breathe, and I could hear the fluid in his lungs gurgling. I immediately took his hand. Next to me was Karen. One of his daughters stood by his feet, and his other daughter held his other hand. His girls were both crying.

They told me that Mitch had a brief moment where he was cognizant. They pulled out a picture of his new granddaughter. Since the baby was so young, she could not travel with them. His daughter blew up a picture of just the baby's face for him. He looked at the picture, but then returned to his prior state of mind. Even so, Mitch was finally able see his granddaughter's eyes that he wanted to see so badly. I was pleased to hear that Mitch's final wish had been met.

I then volunteered to lead a prayer for him. Before I started, I told them all that their father was not in pain. I told them that he had come as a spirit to visit my home, and then I shared the cinnamon story. Given this occurrence, I can say with all of my heart that it was only his shell that was left to struggle. He no longer felt any pain. By looking at Mitch, I could see the eyes of his soul were gone. He was waiting to pass until everyone he wanted was present in the room. I knew that he had total control of when his body would shut down.

Before I continued in prayer, I asked them to repeat after me. We all held hands and said together, "I am at peace, give me peace, I am at peace..." When we finished the prayer, I gave Mitch a kiss on the forehead and asked everyone else to do so after me. I said, "This is the time to say your final goodbyes." I then told Mitch it was his time. I told him his girls would be fine. I gave him permission to go. Immediately after we all had one last opportunity to express our love, Mitch took his final breath.

From the time I entered the room until Mitch took his last breath was less than five minutes. I was amazed how quickly it happened and grateful I was there. More importantly, I was glad I remained so calm for the family. I know I was guided to Mitch before he passed. I also know that I was guided in prayer. I say thank you to everyone on the other side for giving me the strength, poise, and eloquence to lead the prayer during Mitch's final moments.

After we all left his room, we agreed to take turns going back in to be alone with Mitch one last time. The girls went first. Karen, Dale, and I waited in the hallway. Dale had arrived right before Mitch passed without any of us knowing he was there. Karen reminded me that in our last reading, I told Mitch that it would be an honor to help him cross over. I had forgotten about this. No wonder he waited for me to arrive–I had made him a promise. I was sorry it took me so long to get there.

They also told me that when they took a break on the hospice patio earlier that day, there were two redheaded birds. Dale said they did not know what kind of birds they were. Neither Karen nor Dale had ever seen the type of bird before, but they both felt it was a message telling them my father was present. I agreed that it had to be my father. I do not believe it was coincidental that these birds had red heads. We all smiled with gratitude because of such a simple sign, and I said to myself, "Thank you, Dad!"

It was Karen and Dale's turn next with Mitch. The girls and I finally had the opportunity to meet. They expressed their appreciation for me coming. They told me it was amazing how much calmer their dad became once I entered the room.

I needed them to know what I thought of their father. I knew it had been difficult for Mitch to have his daughters live so far away, especially in his last days. I was unsure if they knew what an awesome person he was or how much he loved them, but I wanted to share with them my thoughts. Through my eyes, I said that their father was a man who carried himself with great dignity. I saw him as a man wearing a tuxedo with great pride. They nodded. I told them that it had been my honor to have known their father for such a short period and then thanked them for allowing me to be present with him during his final moments. I hugged them and told them that he wanted both of them to know how much he loved them. I told them that he had not left them, but would always walk with them. They expressed their gratitude to me for being there at such a critical point, especially after he had such poor experiences with prior mediums.

It was now my turn to be with Mitch. I entered the room. I sat next to Mitch holding his same hand that I did when he passed. I could feel his presence in the room. I told him that he was amazing. I told him that I had never experienced someone dying that gave me so much spiritual awareness. I then thanked him for allowing me to be a part of his life and his final moments. I also thanked him for allowing me to feel my father's presence. I would cherish this gift forever. I was unable to be with my father when he died, so I was never able to share any last words with him. I felt like Mitch's process allowed me to mend all of those grieving feelings I had held onto for so long.

I will always treasure the friendship and spiritual connection we shared. During his passing, I felt an indescribable energy that made me feel as if I were closer to heaven, at least for a brief moment. I know that Mitch will always be in my heart. We both learned a tremendous amount from each other in such a short period. I know this is just a new beginning between us.

I ended by telling Mitch that I hope he soared in heaven and received all of the love he deserved. I never felt it was appropriate to say, but while at his bedside, I told him that I loved him. I then kissed Mitch on the forehead one last time. As I walked out the door, I saw the picture of his granddaughter hanging on the wall. I heard Mitch say, "Look at those incredible eyes! I do see life differently now." With that, I smiled and closed the door.

I know that was the last time I saw Mitch in a physical form, but today I can hear him. I know that he is there for me whenever I need him. May God bless you, Mitch.

When I reflect back on everything Mitch endured until his last breath, I can understand why dying is a process. That is, in order to leave this life to pass into the next, one's body needs to struggle to make it through the transition. One could equate it to childbirth. The mother's body is the shell carrying the new child until he or she is ready to be born. The unborn child struggles to push his or her way into this world. Once the child is born, the mother is no longer in pain. As in Mitch's case, his body was a shell. Once the body began to shut down, I believe he no longer felt pain.

I also believe the soul "floats"–it has the ability to be out of the body as well as in the body. The soul can hear and see everything that is happening around them as if from above. When the body is in its final shut down stage, one still has total control to decide when to take a final breath. A person can do this when all of those he or she wants are present and accounted for. In the end, both childbirth and death bring complete peace to a room.

Each individual is different. No one will die exactly the same way as another. That is why we do not have all of the answers for how or when someone will pass. Not all of us will witness our loved ones body go through this struggle in their passing. Many people are comatose until they pass, being highly sedated in order to keep them comfortable. This does not mean their body did not struggle to make the transition. It could be that one is so relaxed that the struggle is virtually undetected.

Whether our loved ones die in a hospital or under hospice, their care should both be the same. I believe that dying individuals should be taken care of with great compassion and detail so that they remain in complete peace and feel no pain during their dying process.

Thanks to hospice, Mitch was able to die in a safe and comfortable place. It gave him a space that felt like his own. He was surrounded with love from his family and friends. Mitch was no longer suffering or wondering. He was now home. I, too, needed to go home. I needed to share my experience with my family and express my love to them.

On my way home, I was again overwhelmed with many emotions. I was happy Mitch was free from pain; I felt sorrow that he had left me. I was in awe over the amazing events that took place. I was anxious to see when, where, and how I would hear from Mitch next.

As I walked through the door, my three-year-old daughter greeted me. She said, "Mommy, where were you?" I explained that I was with a friend who had just died and went to heaven. I told her that he would be with my daddy now. She said, "My daddy is here and your daddy is there, right?" "Yes," I told her. Then she said, "Mommy, my daddy has brown hair and your daddy has red?" Again, I replied, "Yes," but how did she know that? She had never seen a picture of my dad with red hair. Was she seeing him then? Then she said again, "My daddy is here and yours is there. Your daddy is with the angels." She was right. I was so grateful to hear these words—truly out of the mouths of babes. I kneeled down and gave her a big hug. To myself, I thanked her, my dad, and the angels. This was another confirmation that my dad and Mitch were together. I could see them both smiling at me with gratitude. I could hear them say thank you for believing beyond seeing.

✦　✦　✦

May my story of Mitch bring peace and comfort to those of you who have had to witness someone you love die. I hope knowing that they continue to exist in the afterlife brings you peace.

This chapter is dedicated to my dear friend, Richard John Mitchell, "Mitch." I was told he waited a lifetime to meet a medium who was credible. I am sorry it took us so long to meet. I wish I knew him more, but it was not meant to be.

MITCH

(February 15, 1941 to July 5, 2005)

+ 6 +

<u>Messages from Above</u>

AS NOTED IN PRIOR CHAPTERS, spirits send messages in various ways, which can only be received if our eyes and hearts are open to them. Many of us have experienced something peculiar to make us stop and question the occurrence. One could argue if a peculiar circumstance is a mere coincidence or if it could be a message sent to us by a loved one who crossed over.

Examples of such incidents may include your loved ones sending a butterfly, a hummingbird, a dragonfly, or something else appropriate to get your attention and make you think of them. You may also see and feel them in your dreams. You may hear a special song at just the right moment or smell a certain scent that reminds you of them. You may remember them being with you as you wake up from an operation. You may feel a warmth or coolness surround you when you have thoughts of them. You may even notice items in your home misplaced or moved around. These are all signs that let you know your deceased loved ones are around. I call them messages from above.

I personally have witnessed several occasions where deceased individuals sent messages to their loved ones to let them know that they were still around. Below are a few stories. In addition, I included stories from several others because they exemplified the message of this chapter perfectly. Whether you are a believer or not, I sincerely hope these stories will open your eyes and heart to the possibility. I do not believe that these stories are mere coincidences. If you believe, then you too may be able to see all of the messages that are being sent to you.

MARCY

The first story is about my friend Marcy. She came to me for a reading. During our session, Marcy's Aunt Mary came through as a spirit. Through me, her Aunt Mary said that she would send a bird with a red belly to let her know when she was near.

Marcy's Aunt Mary gave the impression during the reading that she often visited Marcy's mother, more than anyone else in her family. Marcy's parents reside in Michigan where the state bird is a robin. Marcy thought to herself that this was a nice symbol, but also common. Therefore, she did not believe that a red-bellied bird would be a clear sign for her.

Weeks later, Marcy and her toddler daughter were in the kitchen playing at their table. While there, a red-bellied bird landed right outside of their kitchen window. They were only five feet away from it. Marcy froze and stared at it. She was afraid to move because she did not want to scare it away. After several moments, the bird remained. Her daughter spun around in her chair and asked, "What is it mama?" Marcy quieted

her daughter and grabbed her camera. She walked up to the window and took pictures of it. She was now only three feet away, and the bird was looking right at her! Marcy was amazed and in awe.

Marcy told her daughter that it was her Aunt Mary letting them know that she was with them. Her daughter did not understand and kept asking, "What, mama?" Her daughter continued watching the bird with delight, as only a toddler could.

Three hours later, Marcy picked up her son from school. The first thing her daughter said to him after he got into the car was, "There was this bird...the angels came to see us!" Marcy had not said anything about angels that day to her, or any other day for that matter. Marcy wondered how her daughter would know to say something like that when she was so young.

Marcy shared with me that she had never been that close to a bird before, particularly one that took notice of her. Marcy also stated that she had never seen this type of bird around her home or neighborhood.

Finally, this story shows that children are not afraid to say what they see. The two of them may have seen a bird together, but one saw it as a sign from her Aunt Mary where the other saw it as an angel visiting. Marcy was fortunate that during our reading she was given a specific sign to watch for. She was then able to see this bird and interpret it as a sign from above. Many of us are not told what type of sign to look for. Given this, we need to be open-minded to what we see, hear, and feel. If we are paying attention and have an open heart, then we can receive the signs from above.

STEPHANIE

In July 2005, I took my oldest daughter, Stephanie, to an orthodontic surgeon. She was scheduled to have her four wisdom teeth removed that day. I went into the surgery room with her. She was nervous, frightened, and uncertain of what was going to happen. This was the first time she would be placed under anesthesia.

We followed the nurse into the room where they prepped her for surgery. My daughter was uncomfortable with needles, so I held her hand and remained by her side. I stayed until she was unconscious. While she was in surgery, I waited in my car and worked. Time flew by. After an hour, I returned to the office to check on her. The nurse told me that the surgery was complete and that she was waking up. I followed the nurse to her room.

Because Stephanie was still heavily sedated, the nurse was having difficulty making her become attentive. As a mother, I had a hard time watching because it looked as though she were severely handicapped. We continued to prod her awake. We then assisted her to another room where she could rest until the anesthesia wore off. The doctor joined us there.

While clearly affected by the anesthesia, my daughter kept uttering that she never went to sleep and did not have the surgery yet. She was adamant about this. The doctor reassured me that her reaction was normal. He told me that she would be fine once she fully woke up. The nurse also told me that girls are typically more emotional coming out of anesthesia than boys are.

After the nurse and the doctor left, we were alone in the room. She looked at me and smiled. She then started crying and said, "My grandfather was here, Mom…he held my hand, Mom…he took care of me, Mom…he said he loved me, Mom." She was speaking about my father. I was pregnant with her when my father passed away. In fact, because the two of them share the same birthday, she always had a strong devotion to him.

She continued, "Mom, he held my hand, Mom, he said he loved me...
he is standing next to you...he combs his hair to the side, he wears
blue pants and a brown belt...where did he go, Mom? I cannot see
him, where did he go?" I calmed her down. I reassured her that her
grandfather is always with her and that she could not see him right
then. I told her to relax so that we could be excused to leave. Frankly,
I was afraid if anyone was listening to us, they would think she was
hallucinating and keep us there longer.

I helped Stephanie into the car. On our way home, she reached down
and held my hand. She told me that my father missed me and loved me.
Given that we were totally alone and could not be overheard, I asked
my father a question. I asked him in my mind if my dear friend Mitch
was with him. Before I could finish my question, Stephanie blurted out
"Red" at that precise moment. As stated earlier, my father's nickname
was Red and Mitch called me Red. My question could not have been
answered any better.

When we returned home, I put her to bed so she could sleep off the
remainder of the medication. Before I went into my office, I realized
that my daughter had just given me my own reading. There was no
doubt in my mind that it was my father who came through that day.
She explained exactly how he combed his hair. He wore blue pants
with a brown belt to work every day. She may have seen a picture of
him with his hair parted, but how did she know about his typical work
attire? I will forever cherish the gifts from that day.

Later that evening when she was feeling better and was no longer
on any medication, I asked her if she remembered telling me about
her grandfather. Stephanie began to cry and responded, "Everything
seemed so real. He was with me. He smiled at me. He told me that he
loved me. He held my hand and helped me, Mom." I gave her a hug
and whispered to her, "Thank you for remembering."

Sometimes our visions from dreams or surgeries seem so real that they are hard to fathom. I believe in my heart that these types of visions are indeed real, albeit on some other spiritual level of our being. Do not be afraid to ask your angels and guides to wake you from your dreams so you can remember who was with you. I suggest that you place paper and a pen by your bedside so that when you wake up, you can write down your dreams when they are most fresh. If you go back to sleep, you may not remember. Then you may miss a message that was intended for you from above.

This was a memorable day for both of us. My daughter was no longer afraid to go under anesthesia. More importantly, she learned that her grandfather was always with her. Every time we talk about that day, she is still overwhelmed and cries. I told her when she feels this way and experiences warmth in her chest or tears in her eyes, she should view it as signs from above. She agreed. To her, this is her grandfather's way of sending her his love.

MICHELLE

My writing partner, Michelle, told me a story that resonates with me and is a perfect example of how a spirit can send a message from above.

It was November 2002, and her ninety-four year old grandmother was in the hospital not expected to live. Michelle grew up with her grandmother only one mile away and was the only granddaughter. Consequently, they had a close relationship that she also told me was more like a friendship.

In her dying days, Michelle asked her grandmother several times, "Nonnie, will you send me a sign and let me know that you are all right when you get to heaven?" Her grandmother was an extremely spiritual woman and replied, "I will do my best to let you know I made it, but I am unsure what I can do from up there. But I'll try...just know that

I'll watch over you." Michelle's grandfather had previously passed, and she knew in her heart that he would be there to greet her grandmother given they were married over sixty years.

On the eve of Thanksgiving, Michelle's mother called to say that Nonnie had passed away just before midnight. Although she knew her passing was imminent, Michelle still cried. She knew it was for the best because now she no longer had to suffer and fight for life, but she could not help but wonder if she was all right.

The very next day, Michelle went to her in-laws for Thanksgiving Day. Michelle put on a pair of embellished jeans that she had not worn in nearly eighteen months due to pregnancy and post-partum weight gain. She was thrilled that they fit again. On the wide-legged cuffs, Michelle had sewn six inches of lace and added her grandmother's antique buttons intermittently around the lace. The lace and buttons also decorated the over-sized pockets in the back. Because her grandmother was a seamstress her entire life, she was particularly fond of the pants given they were so unique and Michelle made them.

Michelle and her family arrived at her in-laws about ten o'clock in the morning. While she and her husband were unloading their car, she walked down the front steps of the home and noticed the beautiful, billowy clouds in the sky. She said that they were gorgeous and huge, the ones you find after a heavy rain. The clouds made her think of her grandmother and if she were in heaven.

While walking down the steps, she put her hands in her back pockets, palms facing out. She then felt something, and pulled out a negative. It was from a 35mm camera, but instead of being part of four negatives in a strip, it was only one by itself. She held up the negative to the sun in order to see what it was.

To her dismay, it was a picture of her mother with her grandmother and grandfather. She knew exactly which picture it was. This picture was about ten years old and was framed in her mother's bedroom. However, her mother's version had only her parents in it. Her mother had cut herself out.

Michelle told me that she was absolutely flabbergasted. She said that she immediately knew that it *had* to be a sign from her grandmother telling her that she made it and was with her grandfather. To this day, she cannot explain how that negative got in her back pocket.

She knew she likely took the picture, but why was it cut from the original strip? She had never made a copy of it. Why did she try on those pants that day and they fit? She had not worn them in months. Could the negative have survived the cleaners? She could not remember when they were last cleaned. Why was she compelled to put her hands in her back pockets backwards at that very moment she was admiring the clouds? She said she never walked around like this. Moreover, it had only been about eleven hours since her grandmother's passing. Could this really be her message, already? These were all questions she told me ran through her head over and over again.

She called her family immediately to tell them what she found. They too were stunned and knew exactly which picture it was. They agreed that it had to be a sign that Nonnie was okay and that she was together again with their grandfather. However, they all questioned Michelle repeatedly how that negative could have possibly landed in her back pocket. Michelle tells me that she is still baffled.

One could argue that all of these circumstances leading up to this negative's discovery were merely coincidences. Michelle and I would argue otherwise. Michelle prefers to think of it as a message from her grandmother. Within hours of her passing, Nonnie had honored Michelle's final wish and came through loud and clear letting her know that she was indeed all right and not alone.

Barbara Guerra with her parents,
Mae ("Nonnie") and Guido ("Poppie") Panighetti

DELORES

Like the story above, I prefer spirits send messages right away to validate their new existence. Signs of validation may include a physical sign, an inner knowing, a feeling, or a healing. My mother, Delores, passed away in December 1984 at the age of fifty-three. My validation did not come until many years later.

Growing up, I never had the chance to know my mother as a typical mother and daughter would. In the twenty-one years we shared together, she lived over fifteen of them with a terrible disease that ultimately took her life. Her body's slow deterioration from her illness unfortunately took away all of who she was and what she represented. It truly stripped her of her dignity.

Being a medium, one may think I can speak to my mother at any time. This is true. However, hearing from her did not happen often, and when it did, I only heard simple things from her. For example, if I asked her, she would help me select jewelry for a special dress or help me decide on how to wear my hair. She would tell me that I was doing well at something, but unfortunately, she never seemed to expand on any topic or have conversations like my father did. Rather, she would just let me know that she was there.

It was a late evening in December 2005, just after Christmas. My sister Cindy and I were sharing our families' Christmas stories over the phone. Since Cindy lived in Wisconsin, we were unable to be together for the holidays. It was also a rare opportunity because it was late at night and no children were present to interrupt our conversation.

As a result, we decided to take advantage of the situation and talk with our father, Frank. Cindy asked him several questions, one of which our grandmother replied to. Then, our mother decided to say a few words—it was the first time ever she had engaged like this. She asked me to ask Cindy if she had any furniture of our parents.

Cindy replied, "Yes, Deb, don't you remember? I have their kitchen table set!" "No," I replied. I said, "I haven't been to your house in years, I must have forgotten." To clarify, I wanted to make sure Cindy knew that it was not me asking her about the table, that it was indeed our mother coming through. Cindy said that she used our parents' kitchen table every day as her main dinner table. My mother then continued, and I said, "Mom is showing me several numbers and the letter 'E.' It is a capital letter 'E.' She is telling me that it is written under the table." I told her that I could see this capital letter "E" extremely clear.

I told Cindy that she would need to get a flashlight and look very closely because the letter and numbers were etched deep into the wood. Cindy checked under the table while I was still on the phone. To her delight, she found "671 E 2404" written on one of the chairs. She noticed it while she was looking underneath the table. We were both thrilled and amazed.

Cindy asked me why our mother wanted her to see these numbers. It was clear to me that my mother gave Cindy a visual validation on the spot so Cindy would believe it was my mother speaking and not me.

My mother gave the two of us the best Christmas present we could have ever received. It was the gift of communication. I then asked my mother why she had waited so long to speak through me. She told me that she often stood behind my father and made him share with me her words. Since I knew my father well, she knew that I would trust in his words. She also told us that she and my father were very close. She said, "His words are my words, and vise versa." She would just tell him what to say to us.

Prior to this, my mother felt that if she spoke through me, I would not have known they were her words. This was because her true personality was overshadowed by her illness during her time on earth. Sadly, I did not know the real her. I am hoping that she will trust in me and talk openly so I can learn more about her. Her spirit that came through that night not only provided us with a glimpse of what she must have been like, but she gave us the yearning to want to know more.

Please note, when spirits interface with me, they reflect the same personality traits that they had while they were here on earth. For example, they may be quiet, talkative, loud, rough, emotional, strong-willed, or humorous. These personality traits help my clients identify their loved ones when I share what I am hearing and feeling.

Based on the above, my mother speaking through my father made perfect sense to Cindy and me since we never had the opportunity to know our mother well. Because she came forward herself that night,

Cindy and I believe that we finally have an opening to get to know her and develop a relationship. We are planning a mother and daughters' day together in hopes that she will come through and open up more. We smile with the possibility of what may happen next.

Moreover, I celebrated my five-year anniversary with my husband this year. To commemorate this milestone, we decided to buy each other rings. Although our anniversary was in September, we did not purchase the rings until December. He chose to upgrade his wedding ring and I selected a beautiful amethyst ring. I chose this ring because I saw the color purple as a color of strength. Knowing I could use extra strength in my everyday life, I thought that this stone would be the perfect reminder.

The rings were ready just before Christmas. We agreed to wrap them and open them on Christmas day. After I opened mine, I put it on. I loved the ring. However, it was only after my phone conversation with Cindy that I learned how special the ring was. An amethyst was February's birthstone, and I realized that my mother's birthday was in February. Even though I selected the ring months prior to Christmas, I believed that my mother guided me to pick the stone. To me, this was another gift from above.

Every time I place the ring on my finger, I feel as though my mother is with me. It is a visual reminder that if I need extra strength, I can count on her. It had been a long time since I felt my mother's love.

Finally, my mother's validation did not end that night. The following morning I received a special Christmas gift from my older sister, Linda. It was a glass jar, which had belonged to our mother. Was this a coincidence? After all of these years, my sister Linda sent me this jar, and I received it just hours after I re-connected with our mother. I truly believe that my mother had something to do with this timing. I will cherish the events of that Christmas forever. I say thank you to my sisters, as well as my mother and father. Every evening I place my rings into this jar before bed.

Before I end this story, Cindy told me that she and her husband often smell coffee at the oddest times. Since both of them are coffee drinkers, they thought nothing of it. Now when they smell it, particularly in the middle of the night, they question themselves. Our mother was a faithful coffee drinker, so when they smell it at unusual hours, they believe it must be our mother saying "hello" and not merely coffee brewing.

✦   ✦   ✦

Spirits can make even a non-believer into a believer. During a reading, one of my clients was told by her father that he would make the lights flicker on Thanksgiving Day. Thanksgiving was her father's favorite holiday. Because she was anxious for this validation, she shared this story with her daughter, mother, brother, and friend. She wanted to ensure that they were all aware so that they did not miss any lights flickering that night. Her brother's response was, "Oh yeah, right!"

She waited all day for her father to affect the electricity as he said he would, but nothing happened. At the end of the evening, she was disappointed. Her brother and friend took their mother back to her apartment at an assisted living place. As soon as they drove up, the entire building's lights were flickering on and off. Her brother told her, "It looked like a Christmas tree!" When they took her inside, the lights there were flickering as well. He could not believe what he was seeing. He immediately called her because he was so excited.

Since that night, she told me that she experienced the most inner peace since her father's death. She wished she could have witnessed these lights for herself, but she understood that her father was watching over her mom, where he needed to be. He told her, "Take care of the love of my life," on his deathbed. It was clear that he was still watching over them from the other side.

When it mattered most, her father came through for them. If he made the lights flicker during Thanksgiving dinner, they may have not believed it was really him. Instead, they may have speculated that it was an electrical shortage given all of the extra electricity being used that day. Her father not only made her a believer, her brother and friend became believers too.

Simply put, our loved ones can play with anything that has a flow of energy–lights, radios, cameras, songs, water, car batteries–to send us signs. When we cross over, our spirit remains a vibrational energy. If spirits want to get our attention, this is one more of their ways to reach us.

Frank ("Red")

We as humans are given five senses. I believe that spirits have the ability to use four of these. Based on my experience, spirits can make us see them, feel them, hear them, and smell them.

My father, Frank, comes to me with the smell of smoke. Although no one in my family smokes cigarettes, I often smell them in my home. Because my father was a heavy smoker in his past life, I have no doubt when I smell smoke, he is nearby.

Some of you may smell other familiar scents such as the scent of a favorite perfume, the whiff of a special flower, the smell of a favorite dish, or your loved one's natural scent. When you smell something out of place that brings back memories, I hope that you will stop and wonder. Maybe someone who loved you is near.

As a child, my father gently rubbed my forehead to relax me so I could fall asleep. Even today, when I need comforting, my father continues to touch my head and let me know that he is there. Many of my clients have voiced to me that they are able to feel their loved ones touch as well. Some say they feel them sitting on their bedside while they fall asleep. Others feel them brush up against them, making their arm hairs stand up straight. Some say when the spirit enters a room it feels like a brisk wind. These gentle nudges from our loved ones' spirits should give us an abundance of comfort and peace because they allow us to know that they are near. I hope you, too, will feel your loved one's touch.

✦   ✦   ✦

The most common question I get is if I can see spirits, and if so, what do they look like? I used to think that if I saw a spirit, I would be scared. As a result, I was unable to see them for a long time. I believe that spirits will not reveal themselves if they feel you are not ready or will fear them. Because I have learned that they are there for good reason, I do not fear them and now see them regularly.

One evening while I was home alone working on my computer, I felt as if someone was behind me. I kept turning around to see if it was one of my children. However, every time I turned around, there was no one there. Even so, I was convinced that there was someone in the room because I felt a strong presence. I decided if I ignored the feeling then maybe it would go away.

I was wrong. I then heard footsteps coming from the back hallway behind me. The sound was coming from my children's rooms. I convinced myself that it had to be my youngest son. However, when I looked in the bedrooms, I saw no one. I returned to my chair next to my computer and faced the hallway. I asked out loud, "Who are you?"

I said, "I know you are there." In an instance, I saw a shadow of a white outline standing in the hallway facing me. I knew that it was a spirit, but was unsure of who it was. I saw no face. It was just an outline of a body figure. Then it disappeared. Since I was no longer hearing or seeing anything, I continued my work.

Later that evening when my youngest son arrived home, I described my experience to him. I gave him a detailed sense of what I felt. I shared my experience with him, not to scare him, but because he seemed to have the same ability to see spirits. He said that he thought he saw this same spirit in the hallway on several occasions. I asked him who he thought it was. After we discussed it for a while, we both speculated that it was a spirit from a reading I did with the lab.

This was a very important reading to me because it was documented research with Dr. Schwartz. It was one of my first readings that proved to me, as well as the lab, that I was capable of interfacing with spirits. In fact, this reading was the turning point that gave me the confidence to pursue what I do because it proved to me, as well as the lab, that I had a special gift.

During the reading, this spirit told me that he would prove that he existed by making noise, revealing himself, or making things move. Although he told me this, I thought that the message I received that day was intended for my sitter. I never imagined that his message was ultimately meant for me.

After considerable thought, I knew this had to be the visiting spirit. When I called him by his name, the spirit ceased, and so did the noise. My son and I were right in identifying him. Whenever I feel his presence to this day, I call him by his first name. He will either stop or talk, or will stop disturbing me once he knows he got my attention.

I now see spirits with no fear. Some appear clearer than others do.

Some are louder than others are. I see them in a shadow of a white light figure. I have seen them walk, sit, stand, and stare at me. Most often, they get my attention through noise. They know I can hear them, yet I do not always want to listen. Therefore, in order to get my attention, they make something happen—it may be a set of footsteps I hear, the TV going on and off, a book falling to the floor, or even an understandable voice that wakes me from a deep sleep. When these events occur, I am caught off guard. However, once they get my attention, they know that I will assist them. I hope that one day you can see or hear a spirit for yourself. It may be overwhelming at first, but if you open your heart to these possibilities, you may receive a message from above.

✦   ✦   ✦

I can only hope that I will continue to receive signs and messages from spirits. They allow me to bring peace from their words to their loved ones in need. I thank all of the angels, guides, and the Highest Divine for granting me this gift, but more importantly, that I have embraced it. May we all continue to grow in the awareness of the spirit world.

+7+

The Future

QUESTIONS ABOUT THE FUTURE OFTEN ARISE during my readings. For example, should sitters ask for predictions or inquire about their future during a reading? If so, are they prepared if the outcome is inconsistent with their hopes? What should sitters do if a spirit sends a message of caution? Should they heed the message and alter their actions? Will the spirits ever lead them astray? Many people feel that if they receive answers into the future, it would give them a sense of peace and comfort. The purpose of this chapter is to give you a reasonable expectation when asking these types of questions.

KRISTINA

During a reading, I may see a red flag flash in my mind. Such a sign symbolizes caution. When I see anything like this, I take the message seriously. Often sitters do not know how to interpret or where to apply it in their life. In fact, they may view it as inconsequential. However, many sitters have later come back to say that they should have trusted what was said and listened.

When I receive a sign of caution from a spirit, the sitters should not view it negatively. Such a message is not necessarily going to change an outcome, but may make the sitters more aware of their situation.

One such example comes from a former client named Kristina. Kristina had recently moved, and many of her boxes were in storage. She was frustrated and upset by the move and called to ask me if I would contact her deceased mother. Kristina wanted me to ask her mother where to find a specific box that contained all of her essential medications.

One of the medications was called Betaseron, an injection therapy for Multiple Sclerosis patients. The other was an anti-depressant medication, which could be dangerous if she missed doses. Kristina knew that she could call her doctor for a refill if need be. However, a refill for just the Betaseron could cost her an upfront fee of more than $1,000 before insurance reimbursement. Being that she was overwhelmed with moving costs, another unforeseen expense was the last thing she needed. As a result, she thought she could ask her mother to assist.

Because Kristina's mother was a pharmacist while in this world, she would know how important these medications were. During our phone conversation, her mother came through immediately. Her mother told me to tell Kristina that the medicine was in a box on the floor. She showed me furniture and the box sitting next to it. Her mother warned not to lift any boxes. She kept saying that she would not need to lift any boxes to find the medicine. She said that if she lifted the boxes, Kristina would hurt her back. She reiterated the box was in an obvious place on the floor.

Kristina was baffled and told me that this did not make sense to her. She said that all of her furniture was on one side of the storage unit and that the boxes were in the back stacked high. She was convinced that there were no boxes on the floor or next to any furniture.

I also told her to look where she was staying. Maybe the box was there and not at the storage unit? She told me that she was staying with her sister and that they had searched the entire house. Once again, I reiterated that the box was obvious and not to lift any boxes. I wished her well and asked her to let me know the outcome.

Later that evening, I received a phone call from Kristina. She found the box full of medications. When we had talked that day, she was at the storage unit and frustrated. When she returned to her sister's home, she saw the box on the floor next to the couch. She, nor her sister, could explain how the box got there. Both of them swear it was not there previously. Could it be that their mother moved it?

Kristina said the key word from her mother was "obvious." When she walked in, the box was blatantly on the floor next to furniture as her mother said it would be. I then asked her, "Did you lift any boxes?" She admitted that she did, which strained her back. She said that she was having a glass of wine to celebrate finding the box and to diminish the pain.

I was relieved to find out Kristina's mother helped her find the box. I was also sorry to hear that during her search she pulled her back. If she had paid attention to her mother's warning, she would have had an even better outcome. For the record, Kristina's back was fine in just a few days.

The red flag I saw was to prevent Kristina from injuring herself. Even though she was given guidance, Kristina chose to ignore the warning. Kristina did not hear "don't lift the boxes;" rather, she focused on the box being in an "obvious place." The lesson from this story was when we receive messages from spirits, we need to pay attention to *all* of their words. They may know something we do not, so it cannot hurt to heed their message.

PETE

With predictions, the big question is, "Will they come true?" Some believe mediums can predict the future, but are we really predicting or are we just manufacturing an outcome? Please note, I am not talking about predictions that affect our world like hurricanes or terrorist attacks. Rather, I am talking about personal predictions, including the following: Will my job remain stable? Is this my soul mate? Will I see my loved one again? Am I going to die before my children or spouse? Such predictions are understandably difficult to answer, but may be given *some* light during a reading. Moreover, I believe if we long for something passionately enough in our minds that we can manifest it to happen.

My client, Pete, was ninety years old when we spoke and had recently lost his wife to cancer. He was married to her for sixty-five years. They never had any children, and all of their friends they had acquired through the years had passed away. He had one living sibling who resided in another state.

Pete contacted me for a reading in order to be reunited with his wife. He wanted to know if she was okay and if she was around him. He also asked me if I could predict when I thought it would be his time to pass so he could be with his wife. He loved her dearly and missed her terribly. I felt the true purpose of our reading was to help Pete understand that his wife was always with him by his side. He just needed to learn how to see signs from her. He needed to finish his journey here on earth and trust that this was a new beginning with his wife watching over him.

Pete's wife came through first saying that she was with her fluffy cat. This message convinced him that it was his wife. She only had one cat in her lifetime, and the cat was extremely fluffy. Second, she told him to buy a cheap plastic hummingbird feeder for the outside patio. She said to place it where he could see it. She said she would send a hummingbird to prove that she still existed and was very much around him.

Pete said afterwards that he felt less alone because the words that were given, he believed, came from his wife. He was excited to see what was going to happen. He said he planned to buy the bird feeder immediately.

Two days after our reading, Pete called. He told me that he placed a plastic hummingbird feeder on the back patio facing his kitchen window. Within twenty minutes of hanging it, a hummingbird appeared. What was more special to him was that this hummingbird did not go to the feeder. Instead, it went to the window and looked directly at Pete. It flew back and forth looking right at him for quite some time.

His wife suggested the bird feeder to help Pete pay attention. Clearly, the hummingbird was coming for him and not the feeder. Pete whole-heartedly believed his wife sent him the hummingbird. Pete told me that he finally understood that she was with him always. Based on this experience, he was excited to watch for other signs from his wife. While I was not able to predict for Pete when he was going to pass, I was able to bring him peace and help him move forward with the days he had ahead of him.

Not too long after, during the writing of my book, Pete passed away and joined his wife. After his funeral services, several friends returned to his hospice center. While we were conversing there, a voice from the television said loud and clear "Pete," and then the television went blank. We all heard this, stopped, and then looked at one another. It was as if this word was uttered by itself so we would all catch it. We concluded that it must have been a sign from him. He showed me that he was thrilled to be with his wife again. Perhaps one day he will send me a hummingbird too.

DIANA

Dr. Schwartz asked me to do another blind reading. I did not know the place, the sitter, or the spirit. I began the session with a male spirit. Soon thereafter, a strong woman spirit appeared to me. I asked Dr. Schwartz if I should digress from the current spirit to speak with her. He encouraged me to do so.

I described to him a tall, blonde, slender woman with high cheekbones. I said she was angelic looking and very beautiful. What stood out the most was her smile. It was her most significant feature.

Dr. Schwartz then asked me about her hobbies. I saw both water and snow skiing. She loved art. I then told him I saw she died in a car accident. She seemed relatively young, as if her life was cut short. She was visibly upset that her life ended in such a tragic manner. She felt that it should not have been her time and she left this world too soon. Her life's work was incomplete.

Dr. Schwartz then asked me if she knew Susy Smith, and my head nodded "yes" automatically. Because Dr. Schwartz experienced this woman's spirit in other medium readings, he told me that she was famous. It was then that I saw her clearly. It was Princess Diana in her wedding dress, clear as a bell in my mind. She then showed me one of Dr. Schwartz's books. She also showed me that she was mad at him by throwing his book.

We soon learned why she seemed so aggravated. In Dr. Schwartz's experience with Princess Diana, when she opened up to mediums, she presented herself as an ordinary individual. She waited until she gained trust in the medium before she revealed herself. If she showed herself too soon, then a medium may get caught up in her "famous former life" and not take her seriously. Given that Dr. Schwartz was a scientist and skeptic by nature, she was frustrated that he kept questioning if it was really her. The purpose of our blind reading was to prove that Princess Diana would come through again, and she did. Our session ended soon thereafter, but I could not believe what had just transpired.

Months later, the day before he was to travel to England for a seminar, Dr. Schwartz called to ask me if he would be receiving any messages from Princess Diana. Through me, Princess Diana said that he would receive signs as messages from her. She told me that he would need to be present in each moment and pay attention so he could see the signs.

Princess Diana also told me to tell him to say "hi" to Hazel Courteney, a dear friend of his. Hazel Courteney was an award-winning health columnist that specialized in alternative health and spiritual issues in the United Kingdom. She was with The Sunday Times in London and had spoken with Princess Diana on several occasions.

I was familiar with Hazel, but had no idea that Dr. Schwartz planned to see her while he was in England. He then told me that not only would he be seeing her, he was staying at her home for part of his trip. He just finished talking to her on the phone prior to our call. Clearly, Princess Diana was giving Dr. Schwartz a message during our phone conversation so that he would be convinced she would send him messages in England.

When he returned from his trip, he called to share with me the messages he received while in London. First, he stayed at a hotel that turned out to be a short walk from her memorial called "Diana, Princess of Wales Memorial Fountain, Hyde Park, London." Not only was the hotel location symbolic, Hazel told him that the restaurant there at the hotel was where she had met Diana for lunch. To quote Dr. Schwartz and Susy Smith's favorite line, "It was too coincidental to be accidental."

I truly vacillated if I should share this Princess Diana story in my book. Moreover, because it was a research reading to collect data on this particular subject, I had to ask Dr. Schwartz for permission to reveal this information. I was pleased he gave me his blessing to include this experience. I realize that this story may be difficult for some to comprehend, but it was based on genuine research and validated information.

I believe Princess Diana will continue to help others in this life as well as the next. Not to belittle her time on earth, but Princess Diana wants to be known as a "normal" living soul in the afterlife, not the famous person she was. She too has an agenda similar to our loved ones. She wants to re-connect with her family and friends, watch over and help others, and send messages confirming that she still exists.

To summarize, did I predict for Dr. Schwartz something that would happen in the future? Or did I give him guidance from Princess Diana to watch for messages? I prefer to think of it as the latter. She did not tell him what the signs were going to be. Rather, Princess Diana told him to pay close attention and to remain in the moment. Because he was clearly aware, he saw her signs. As a result, Dr. Schwartz said that he was pleasantly surprised with her messages during his England visit.

For further information about this research, Dr. Schwartz shares an afterlife experiment and reading done for Hazel Courteney about Princess Diana in *The Truth about Medium*.[7] This experiment used two different mediums to contact Princess Diana through blind readings. The results were "breathtaking," to quote Dr. Schwartz from his book. Hazel's book, *The Evidence for the Sixth Sense,* also addresses this topic at length.[8] Studies and experiments continue with Princess Diana, amongst other famous individuals. I am blessed to be a part of such intriguing research projects.

JULIE & JENNIFER

It was a sunny Friday afternoon in September. My friend Julie had called asking if I could receive a message from her mother that she could give to her sister Jennifer. Jennifer was going to be married the following Sunday. Julie thought it would be nice if Jennifer received words from her mother for her wedding day.

Julie's mother expressed to me that she would be with Jennifer to guide her through her special day. Her advice was to smile for her pictures, enjoy each moment, and please ask her for assistance if she felt frustrated or nervous. She specifically stated to Julie that Jennifer was going to be confused about which lipstick to wear out of two. She said to tell Jennifer to use the second choice. She ended our session with feelings of joy and love for both of her daughters. She reiterated that she would be there all day and would not miss a beat.

On Sunday, while getting ready, Julie told her sister Jennifer that she had some messages from their mother. As Julie was getting her notes, Jennifer came out of the bathroom and asked Julie which lipstick she should use out of two. Julie said she smiled, advised her to select the second one, and then shared their mother's messages.

As insignificant as it may seem to select a lipstick color, this incident made all of the difference in Jennifer's belief. She was able to know in her heart that her mother was not going to miss her wedding day after all. How could a spirit know that lipstick choice would be an issue at such an appropriate moment? Although we will never know the answer, it can be considered a prediction that was ultimately given for peace and comfort.

✦   ✦   ✦

I often wonder when a sitter asks a spirit to predict an outcome, if they want this answer from me or the spirit. When I am asked to relay these types of questions, I typically turn them into a question for my client. For example, if I am asked, "Will my relationship sustain?" I then ask, "Do you feel your relationship is doing well?" I may need to ask several more questions until my client feels they have received an answer they were looking for.

Not surprisingly, the answer often comes from them answering their own questions. They do not always realize that they have all of the answers deep within themselves. My advice is to keep a journal chronicling any deep feelings regarding these questions. The answers in time should surface naturally.

I mentioned earlier in the chapter how I believe one can manifest events to happen in life. For example, if people desire more money so they can be financially secure, then they may pray for it to happen. The spirits, guides, and Highest Divine may send money, as they deem appropriate, through various channels. The money may come through a gift, a more lucrative job, or an opportunity for overtime. If this is the case, then the desire to have more money can only happen if the person is open and willing to save their money, accept the job change, or work more hours. A person must *be* the flower and attract the butterfly rather than search for the butterfly.

I also think these desires must be qualified with "if it is in the highest and best good." A person must be careful when asking questions about the future—he or she must understand exactly what is requested and why. After this, paying close attention to the spirits' messages is the key. Unfortunately, many read into messages and create answers that the spirits never said. People notoriously hear only what they want to hear, and therefore lose the true meaning of the messages.

✦ 8 ✦

Science and Skepticism

IN THE PREVIOUS CHAPTER, THE FUTURE, I discussed the validity of predictions. That chapter serves as the perfect segue into this chapter, Science and Skepticism. Simply stated, scientists want to challenge predictions and their outcomes while skeptics want to equate them to hogwash.

For me, science and skepticism should be defined the same way. Both function under the notion of black and white, with little room for grey. Scientists and skeptics need to have cold, hard facts to prove, or disprove, their beliefs. As a result, it is not unusual that I am often confronted about my beliefs, my sixth sense abilities, my accuracy, the existence of an afterlife, as well as the purpose and validity of my work.

Because the ordinary person cannot see, hear, feel, taste, or smell this afterlife world, it is indeed a difficult case to prove. On the one hand, a skeptic may receive pertinent and accurate information from me during a reading, but equate it with coincidence or luck. On the other hand, a scientist may receive a similar, accurate reading from me, but will endeavor to decipher and interpret all of the facts to discover the truth.

Based on scientific experiments, if random persons were to guess at a reading, they average about five to ten percent in accuracy. If this is true, then are my readings, that have been tested to be proven eighty to ninety percent accurate, merely coincidences?[9] Or, am I one of the blessed individuals that has a sixth sense that allows me to tap into this other phenomenal world?

As noted previously, Dr. Gary Schwartz is a professor of psychology, medicine, neurology, psychiatry, and surgery at the University of Arizona. He is also the director of the Laboratory for Advances in Consciousness and Health. One focus of his ongoing studies is the VERITAS Research Program, which investigates the survival of consciousness after death by collecting large amounts of data under controlled laboratory conditions. His lab's motto is, "If it is real, it will be revealed. If it is fake, we will find the mistake." I consider Dr. Schwartz a scientist by degree and a skeptic by nature.

As a medium, I was honored to be selected to participate in Dr. Schwartz's afterlife experiments. Dr. Julie Beischel, Assistant Director of the VERITAS Research Program, selected me after an interview and test reading. Through the lab's experiments, several of my readings were recorded, documented, and scored. Based on my accuracy, the lab allowed me to dispel my own skepticism. I gained validation and credibility from the lab that what I heard from spirits was relevant, intriguing, valuable, and profound. Since my initial work with the lab, I have passed (as of June 2006) a portion of the rigorous nine screening steps required by the VERITAS Research Program. The steps are described in *Integrated Medium Research: Scientific and Spiritual Opportunities and Guidelines for Mediums and Researchers*.[10] The steps are a lengthy process, but I hope to complete them within the year.

Through these experiments amongst many others, Dr. Schwartz has collected enough positive data to abandon his skepticism. He has published hundreds of scientific papers on various topics and is the author of several books including *The Afterlife Experiments*[11] and *The*

Truth about Medium.[12] Both of these books explore and answer questions about the afterlife, and in particular, whether we can communicate with the dead.

To test their hypothesis, Drs. Schwartz and Beischel have tested mediums through single-, double-, and triple-blind readings. For a single-blind reading, the medium does not know, see, hear, or receive any feedback from the sitter. However, the medium may be given the first name of the sitter or deceased. They may also be given the relationship of the deceased to the sitter in order to focus the reading. Again, the sitter and medium have never met. Despite this fact, sitters are told they may invite their loved ones to be present for their reading. When a single-blind reading is scored, sitters know the reading was intended for them because they typically hear the reading from behind a partition in the room or silently on a phone line.

To make an experiment double-blind, mediums are still blind to the sitter like in a single-blind reading, but a "proxy" sitter (usually an experimenter) sits in so that the sitters do not hear the reading. Even though the sitters do not participate in the reading, an experimenter may advise the sitters to think of their loved ones and invite them for the reading. After the reading is completed, the information is transcribed for later scoring by the sitters. Because the sitters do not hear the reading, they are given two legitimate readings to review (one intended for them and one intended for another sitter) and must select one as their own in addition to scoring it.

For a triple-blind experiment, there is a proxy sitter like in the double-blind method, but to take it one step further, the experimenter acting as the proxy sitter is also blind to any information about the sitter or the deceased. The experimenter is simply given the name of the deceased by a research assistant. This is the only information the experimenter knows and therefore can share with the medium.

Simply put, the triple-blind approach is summarized as follows: 1) the mediums are blind to the identities of the sitter and their deceased loved ones, 2) the sitters are blind to which readings are theirs, and 3) the experimenter is blind to the identities of the sitters and deceased and any specific information related to them, aside from the first name of the deceased. With the experimenter being blind and no sitter involved, the possibility of telepathy or mind-reading is mitigated.

Moreover, given such controlled circumstances, the likelihood of an accurate reading based on chance or guessing is reasonably decreased. Correspondingly, that is why the results are so significant. If mediums score well in such situations, then they provide valuable evidence supporting the hypothesis that there is life after death.

Below is the exact dialogue from a triple-blind reading I performed for the VERITAS Research Program. Drs. Schwartz and Beischel designed the specific protocol together, although Dr. Beischel acted as the experimenter and performed all of the steps of this particular study. It is with their permission that I am able to share this research with you.

Date: 12/10/04

Discarnate: Donald
Medium: Debra Martin

M = Medium
E = Experimenter (Dr. Julie Beischel)

> E: *The discarnate's first name is Donald, but he also goes by Don. So for Part A, we'll just see what information we can get from Donald.*

M: I see Donald—I feel Donald as a very calm, um, relaxed person, like when he's in the room you feel very, um— he kind of makes the room feel very… very good, very positive, very, um—when he talks to you, he's very calm. Um… he's one that is—he would make sure he's very careful with his words, um, careful in the fact that, you know, he's… he's… how do I say this?… Um, he's a gentle soul. He's gentle with his words. Um, so he would be caring. Um… he… I see tall, like a tall man. Um… let's see. What else?

Um… I just feel like when he, like—I can't explain— like when he's in the room, like he's sitting here in this room, there's a part of you that just feels very, like, very taken care of, um… that you know everything's gonna be okay… That's kind of what I see with him. Um… and he's just not going to say anything just to—you know, he's going to be very specific, if you want to ask questions.

E: *Do you want me to go on to the questions then?*

M: Yeah.

E: *Okay. For Part B, the Life Questions, the first question is what does the discarnate look like? Give a physical description of him including relative height, build, and hair color, if possible.*

M: I see very tall; tall meaning almost 6 feet. It's six feet he's saying. Um, lighter hair. Um… not that it's blonde, but it's lighter. So it's just lighter hair, he says, just lighter hair. Um… and blue eyes. Um… now he's kind of chuckling, so he has a kind of—he has a humor to him and he's, you know—he's showing me himself as tall and slender, however, when he passed, he was not slender [laughs]. And not saying he was fat, he was just on the heavier—you know, he was, um, he—now on this side of life he could—on the other side of life he could show you—in the afterlife, he can show—he can represent whatever he wants. And he's going to look slender and handsome. So, um, it's what he would have liked to stay at this weight in his, in his, um, earth life here. Okay.

E: *Number 2 is: describe the personality of the discarnate including whether he was more shy or more outgoing, more serious or more playful, and more rational or more emotional, if possible.*

M: Um, he's one of the characters that you laugh a lot, 'cause he's making me laugh. Um, my face already is like, um… laughing. Like he'll put a twist on everything. Um, he has this kind of humor where, um, he has this kind of humor where, um, he just makes everybody laugh. He, in the room—you know how I said it's calm when he's in there?—but he also can take over the room and just make it—he doesn't mind being center of attention. Um… in fact, he enjoys center of attention, center of conversation, he's good at conversation, he's good at, um, the humor. Um… I wouldn't call him shy at all. Um… when I said he was quiet earlier—or I didn't say he was quiet, I said he was calm—okay, he does—he is being very specific before with his words because this is very important. However, um, he wasn't afraid to talk when he was here. Um, and yeah, he's just one of these people that will always make you laugh, always—I have a smile on my face the entire time. He'll keep you with a smile on your face as long as he's with you.

E: *Okay. What were the hobbies or activities of the discarnate during his life? What did he like to do?*

96

M: Hobbies… He's got me smiling, so I'm trying to figure it out. It's like funny to him, to think of it as a hobby, is what he's saying and I don't know what he means by that. Um… he fussed a lot with different things, "fussed," "fussed," I'm trying to hear what he's saying… um… no tools, 'cause I was going to ask him if he liked tools. No tools. Um… cars, he's showing me cars, so he liked cars, so it's not anything—no tools, so he didn't fix cars, but he had a hobby of liking cars. Um… And… he's being playful, so I don't know if it's playful with children. Yes, children. Very playful. Um, his hobby would be to spend time with them. I don't know if this is, um, grandchildren or his children, I just see children. Um… and he liked to spend time—let's see what else he liked to do….

Um, yard, mowing the yard, was always, um, kind of therapeutic for him, he didn't mind it at all, um… In fact, he says he enjoyed it. He may have griped about it, but he did enjoy it. Um… I'm just asking questions, in my mind, like "pool?" He says "no pool."

E: *Like swimming pool?*

M: Mm-hmm [affirmative]… I would just leave it at that.

E: *Okay. And then the fourth question is what was his cause of death?*

M: …Just sudden. Um… I'm feeling kind of like… um, my upper chest hurts. Like by my throat more, like the upper, upper, not my lower chest, my upper chest. Um… I think that there was swallowing, 'cause it feels as if my throat is, um, swelling up. So it would be like—I don't know if he drowned, you know, drowned of his own, um, you know, like if he—if it was some type of car wreck or something where all of the sudden, you know, like he's hit and then they, they drown of their own fluids. 'Cause I'm feeling something with—It was quick, sudden, and his throat filled up. Um... and... it was not a car accident. "I never said that." Um, this was very... 'Sudden' can also mean that, is what he's explaining to me, is this happened rather quickly what he—what was happening to him. You know, he could be in his, in his bed, you know, hospital bed, and that was what happened to him at the end, um, because they told me he did—they did have last words, and he wants this woman, this special woman—that's what he calls her: special—in his life to know that he heard all her words. She wasn't sure and, um... that's why, you know, sometimes they hang on or if he'd said that he struggled dying or anything like that, it was one of these things that was sudden and this all happened rather, you know, quickly. But sometimes then when somebody is saying their last words, they—he may have been with his—you know, like comatose or something, you know, with—on meds—and she doesn't know if he heard them. And he did. He even heard words once he passed on, he was still in the room. And it's kind of like this is for healing for her again it's like just saying, um, he did hear everything. Um... and it was—if she needs to know—it was painless. It sounds awful, you know, that that has to happen, where you—with something with your throat filling up and everything but it was painless for him. Okay.

E: *And then the last part is the Reverse Question, so does Donald have any comments, questions, or requests for the sitter?*

M: Um... I don't know why he says clean out the fridge [laughs]. He makes you laugh again, so I don't know where that comes from. Um, clean out the fridge, so obviously it might need to be cleaned out or may be that's something he always told her. She'll know what the connection is. Um, clean out the fridge. That's his humor again. Um... He shows me a picture of himself... it must be on the night stand... and, um, he's there every time she looks at it, she can talk to him because he's—it's like he's looking through those eyes and he sees her and he hears her. It's almost like it gives her a place of knowing where he's at and that would be in that room, um, which would be—there must be lots of—she must feel him a lot in the bedroom, 'cause he's feeling "bedroom." Um... it's just the closeness is in there. It's not that, he's not always just in that room, but that's where she feels him the most. Um... yeah, I just see this picture, um... Honor... my life. Honor my life—what is he trying to say?—honor my... um... He's trying to say something. Live through... no... honor my... (you know it, you know it...) honor my... honor my life... by... living... yours. Honor my life by living yours. I think what he's trying to say is... by you going on in life will honor his. Does that make sense? Um... honor my life by living yours, I think that's the words he wants, it just took awhile to get there.

Um... love, love, love. Three love's, which means he stresses love very much, there was very much love and there still is, and it never goes away and it's for ever lasting and, um... you need—that's what life's about, so love, love life to the fullest. Um... when he says love, also, it's like, they had so much love, there is so much love, and every—life is about love. So, those three things I just said plus, you know, love again, love again. Life is about love. That's like five loves: love again, love life... I can't repeat the last—the three that he just said, 'cause I don't remember exactly, but if you go back to the tape, you'll hear each one, what it meant. And he underlines the words, so they're just—they're very strong from him and between the sitter and him. It was very, very strong.

Um… he has no regrets. And he loved—He, um, had a happy life and there isn't anything he'd do over. And he says "She'll think, 'Yeah, right. That's wrong, he would have done a couple things over.'" But what he's saying is truly what really mattered, he wouldn't have done over. She'd say "Oh, that's wrong, that's wrong, because he would have done a few things differently," and he's saying no, if you look at the things that matter, everything was done—he wouldn't have changed it.

Um… He's also saying that the person that is the sitter will be very critical, um, because this person Donald is so close to her and she has to be critical because it has to be—because she wants to make sure it's really him. And um, he asks her to read this several times, not in one sitting. He wants her to read it, he wants her to place it down, and maybe go back to it—like once in the morning, once at night—and different things will pop out at her. The sitter really needs to take the time and, um, she'll see what is right and what is wrong, but because she is so critical, if she doesn't open herself up, she won't see it, 'cause she's seeing everything so black and white. She needs to take—she needs to do this, not just do it once, she needs to do it a couple times… and then the words will be there. She's also very—she'll also going to be very nervous. As much as she wants this, she'll be very nervous because the person means a lot to her. And he's there, he will help her through this. But he wants her to know, he will help her through this. It's going to take a couple times for her [laughs]. Okay.

E: *That's all I have unless you have anything else.*

M: No, I think he really went through his—what meant the most to him. And, like I said, he is one that will put a smile on everybody's face as soon as you walk into the room or through the door.

100

E: Okay. Well, we will thank Donald and thank Debbie and turn the recorder off.

As a side note, I am a bit embarrassed about the numerous "Ums" included above. I would have deleted them, but I wanted this reading to be authentic, exactly as it happened. As I process information and symbols to obtain messages, it is not unusual that I fill the void in conversation with "Ums" to help me get my thoughts together. However, it was with this reading in print (amongst others) that I realized how often I do this. I have since strived to eradicate this useless word from my vocabulary!

So with "Ums" aside, the sitter then blindly rated the experiment using the following rating scale:

6- Excellent reading, including strong aspects of communication, and with essentially no incorrect information

5- Good reading with relatively little incorrect information

4- Good reading with some incorrect information

3- Mixture of correct and incorrect information, but enough correct information to indicate that communication with the deceased occurred

2- Some correct information, but not enough to suggest beyond chance that communication occurred

1- Little correct information or communication

0- No correct information or communication[13]

According to the experimenter, the sitter blindly, yet correctly, chose the above reading as her own and then scored it as a "5" on the above scale of 0-6 (speaking to accuracy). We were all pleased with my results.

✦   ✦   ✦

Many people question if we should contact, or disturb, this spirit world. They question whether there are good spirits or bad spirits. They wonder how these sprits see us now. My view is if it were not okay to contact the spirits, then they would not be able to engage me to hear them, see them, feel them, and smell them.

My purpose in life is to share the contact I receive from them with those who are grieving here so they all achieve comfort and peace. Again, I am only a messenger. I try to deliver the messages I receive as precisely as I can. I am only a link between two worlds where messages are sent via tidbits of information and symbolism for intended individuals. Such information from a spirit to a loved one is meant to dispel their myths, fears, or stigmas about the existence of the afterlife. The spirits want them to know that they are all right and that they are present to assist them during their trials and tribulations.

✝　　✝　　✝

Although I have touched upon many readings in this book, I would like to take the time to walk you through a typical reading, from start to finish, from my perspective.

First, more than ninety percent of my readings are done over the telephone. This allows the sitter to be in a comfortable safe setting and prevents our reading from being overshadowed about judgments of me, my office, the surroundings, etc. If clients are skeptic or apprehensive, I feel that I process less information from their loved one. The more open-minded they are, the more I can receive.

Like the laboratory studies, I do not know who the sitter is the majority of the time. I am often contacted via email or phone from people that found me on the Internet, heard about me from a friend, saw my name on the VERITAS website, or caught a glimpse of me on television. I do not need to see the sitter to get accurate information. In fact, it is not unusual that the sitter is from out of state. I have even done readings from my home in Arizona to such countries as Australia, England, and Canada to name a few.

I typically know the sitter's name, simply from phone conversations or emails. Unless it is for research, it is irrelevant if I know the names or not. For the readings, I then ask who they hope to contact. I ask specifically for the loved ones' names so I can begin to receive messages from them.

A skeptic might argue that I should not be given *any* information at all so that I can see who comes through naturally. This is true for controlled laboratory settings. As described above, I am not given any clues, significant instructions, or relative feedback. I never meet or see the sitter. After an experiment has ended and is scored, it is then that I can find out the accuracy of my reading.

Once I know the spirits to contact, I channel them to obtain pertinent information for the sitter. I usually begin to recognize specific sights, sounds, and feelings from the deceased living soul. This can be days before our meeting time. The spirits are usually very much alive and playful when they speak through me. Again, their personality traits will come through. They may be funny, stubborn, stern, reserved, persistent, or even bossy.

I personally take on their feelings, emotions, and mannerisms. I may feel ecstatic because they are thrilled to speak with their loved one. I may feel sorry or ashamed for something they did. I may even cry. I may pace. I may tap my foot to show nervousness. I also may laugh out loud at words that do not have meaning to me, but hold significance to the sitter. I may feel compelled to clean, only because they were a neatnik. My knees may hurt, because they had arthritis in them. They may still feel a need to tell their loved one how to do things their way. These are all examples of how they define themselves for their loved ones. The sitters must then make the connection between my messages and their memories of them.

Also, if they had an accent, I may speak as though I came from New York, Texas, England, etc. I will reflect their accent to validate them. Again, I do not ask or know this sort of information before a reading, so when an accent comes through, it is unsolicited and spontaneous. I allow them to take over and communicate in their familiar style.

During a reading, the sitters involve themselves by asking questions and interfacing with me regarding the messages given. Once this happens, then it becomes easier for me to engage the spirit and receive additional information. It is as if the sitter, the spirit, and I all need to get into a rhythm and develop a trust, which allows the information to flow freely amongst us.

Note, if I have more than one spirit coming through, I write their names on individual pieces of paper and take notes from the appropriate spirits, keeping them in line. I realize this may sound confusing, but in an unexplainable way, the spirits are patient and systematic. They either show me their name, as if a vision in my head, so I know to place their sheet in front of me. Or, I will ask them to step forward in order to take notes. However, if they are anxious and speak out of turn, they then need to show me their name in order to re-direct my focus.

Although the spirits may share recognizable memories with the sitter, they may also tell us things that are unknown or unfamiliar to the sitter. In these situations, a sitter may have to follow-up and confirm with a friend or family member to validate the spirit's message. In fact, I have had spirits contradict the sitter only to discover later that the spirit was right and the sitter was wrong. In these situations, I feel vindicated because with each reading I realize that I have to accept the possibility of being wrong or the possibility that others may not believe in me.

In addition, when the deceased gives details perplexing to the sitter, and the sitter researches and validates the message later, I also believe that the information becomes more valuable and meaningful. I say this because often times a skeptic will think a medium can read a sitter's mind. This exercise proves that the message given was unknown to both the medium and the sitter. It is only after the research that the sitter can make the logical and viable connection to what was said.

Before I engage with a spirit for a reading, I remove myself from all distractions. I have trained myself to ignore my own consciousness so that I know the words I am receiving are not my own. I also do not drink for up to twenty-four hours before a reading. I typically experience butterflies in my stomach before each reading. The unknown of what is to come can be unsettling because each reading is unique and I never know what is going to happen.

I then sit quietly and pray. I give permission to the living souls to communicate through me. I ask my guides, angels and the Highest Divine to assist and direct me so that I am allowed to hear, feel, see, and smell what they need in order to relay their message. I ask the angels for strength, communication, and healing. I ask them to surround the reading with light and love. In order to give all of my clients an experience that will leave them with a sense of peace and comfort, I pray all of this and more.

Because I take my gift seriously and I want to insure I treat all of my clients equally, I stand by my personal code of ethics. It represents all that I am as a medium. It is as follows:

Integrity- Honor oneself and the afterlife as a medium.

Truth- Portray my work in the most honest and positive light.

Compassion- Be compassionate to everyone I serve.

Honesty- Always be true to the afterlife, my client, and myself.

Fairness- Show patience and understanding toward all clients, even if they disbelieve what comes through.

Ethicality- Embrace principled values and make no judgments on another.

Responsibility- Be a positive role model for the profession of mediums.

Cooperation- Collaborate with other mediums and do not slander another.

Spiritual Values- Remember my gift comes from the Highest Divine—I must never misuse or abuse it.

Respect- Demonstrate respect toward all people I serve, here and in the afterlife.

Love- Make love the foundation for all of my work.

My readings average about one hour, although I have had them last up to four hours. Readings are done when the spirits withdraw and the communication subsides. I allow the spirits to dictate my readings to allow sufficient time for what they think needs to be said.

Again, my job as a medium is to be a messenger. I only relay the information I am given for each particular sitter. I am human, so I cannot be 100% accurate all of the time. Certainly, I would like to be for my own ego and for my clients, but this is impossible. My job is to convey the information as best I can, no matter what is said or what purpose it serves.

It is also important to note that occasionally I do not receive any "pre-information" from the spirits and it is only after a reading begins that I begin to process and receive information.

Being a medium, I do not go into my office and know what to expect each day. There is simply no guidebook for this line of work. Because each medium has his or her own technique, there is no right or wrong way. We learn as we go from all of our experiences.

For me, I walk with all of my senses open to the spirits throughout my days and believe that whatever needs to be said will be said. I am vulnerable each day and with each reading because I want to be as accurate as possible. On days where I receive little information or a reading does not go as I had hoped, I feel devastated. I feel this way because I want to receive information that will touch my clients and provide the ultimate experience for them. I want them to walk away with a new beginning with their loved one. I do my job out of pure love and with good intentions for all involved. Given this, I am naturally saddened when I cannot obtain the same high level of results for all of my clients.

BIANCA

I would like to share with you a reading I did for a sitter in another state whom I had never met before. I was asked on several occasions if I could perform a reading for a sitter if his or her loved one only spoke another language. I had no idea because I had never attempted it. I discussed this notion with my writing partner and said that it is something I should test for my own knowledge. Since I call upon Archangel Gabriel to assist with the communication of the messages in my readings, I thought she would be ideal to call upon for translation needs.

My writing partner, Michelle, volunteered a family friend who was from Italy. Her name was Bianca and she resided in California. All I knew about Bianca before the reading was her name, her approximate age (about seventy), that she was Italian, she was bilingual, and the names of the two Italian individuals she hoped to contact. One was her mother, Josephina, and the other was her dear friend, Anna.

When Michelle called her to confirm the reading time, Bianca inquired, "How will Debbie speak with them?" Michelle told her that I planned to call Archangel Gabriel to assist in the translation. Bianca then said, "I have worn the medal of Gabriel around my neck for many years..." Michelle viewed this as a positive sign for our reading and was excited to relay this message to me.

Then, the day before the reading, I was contacted by Susy Smith. I was reading Dr. Schwartz's *The Afterlife Experiments* and read that Susy Smith talked with Dr. William James and wrote a book about it called *Ghost Writers in the Sky*.[14] Dr. James was a Harvard professor of psychology and philosophy and was the first president for the American Society of Psychical Research. After I read this, Susy led me to my computer and asked me to Google the book. I am not sure how I got to the particular site, but it was to purchase *Ghost Writers in the Sky*. On the webpage, it allowed me to browse the book. Susy directed me to pages 45 and 46. The following is what she guided me to read:

> *"To some new arrivals, James says, language is initially a barrier. Advanced spirits have learned to communicate entirely by telepathy, and they can talk with citizens from any country on earth or any other planets in the universe. 'But when you first enter the Etheric you are*

untrained to use your thoughts in this manner. You are told how to employ telepathy, but it usually takes some time to assimilate this information and put it to use. So if you wish to take advantage of an interchange of ideas and information with those of other countries, you may find it expedient to spend some time studying a foreign language. You will discover real pleasure in becoming bilingual or trilingual."[15]

The timing of Susy leading me to this quote the day before my bilingual reading was the perfect reassurance. I knew it was a sign, but was uncertain what it meant and if we would encounter communication issues during our meeting. Even so, I was excited to perform the reading.

Below are excerpts from our session. Bianca and I were both ultimately encouraged by the results. For me, I learned that spirits transcend the language barriers, or maybe it was Archangel Gabriel hard at work? Or perhaps Josephina and Anna are "advanced spirits?" Nevertheless, it was a learning experience for both of us, and I am grateful to Bianca for assisting me with such an endeavor. The following highlights parts of our conversation and is a prime example of how a typical reading proceeds.

We started the reading with the personality of Bianca's mother. Josephina was very stern, bossy, proper, motherly, but at the same time, funny, loving, and warm. According to Bianca, my experience with her mother was on target.

D = Debra
B = Bianca

> *D: Your mother is very funny… everything has to be fresh, fresh, fresh, like fresh linens. Everything has to be clean, like I felt like I wanted to clean all morning. Your mother*

is funny because as you get ready and as I got ready, she is always very particular, she says to always look your best, take your time getting ready, when you do your hair, your makeup, always do your best for the day, I wasn't sure if I was...

B: You hit it right on the nail.

D: *Did I? (Laughing.) That is the time you take your time.*

B: Yeah, you're right.

We then spoke with her best friend, Anna. She was grateful for the flowers Bianca brought to her. It will be interesting to see if Bianca's rose bush experiences its best year ever.

D: *Anna says to you thank you for the flowers. Did you plant a bush, because I see a bush that produces flowers?*

B: Every time I went to Italy, I went to the cemetery [and put flowers there for her].

D: *She says thank you. That is what she is thanking you for. She is aware of it. She sees it and says thank you. That is very nice of her.*

B: She was (inaudible).

D: *She is smiling right now. When she smiles, her cheeks are very round. Do you have a rose bush?*

B: Yeah, I have a rose bush.

D: *Okay, because she thanks me for the flowers, but then she shows me this bush—of course it is not a bush by the cemetery, but you gave her flowers—so she is thanking you for the flowers you gave her. But she is also showing me this rose bush. So that is why I ask if you have one and you say you do in the back yard. Could you please watch it this year watch how it blooms and if it blooms better than it ever has. That is because she is giving you flowers back.*

B: Ok.

D: *So pay attention, that will be neat to watch.*

We then discovered a long lost treasure that Josephina wants Bianca to dust off and bring out of the closet. It was a bedspread that had belonged to her mother. Josephina would love to see Bianca display it so she can think of her whenever she sees it.

D: *I see a beautiful quilt... I don't know, is it a quilt? I don't know if you call it a quilt, or a blanket, it is something beautiful, beautiful... Is it something that was hers?*

B: I have a bedspread that was hers...

D: *Bedspread, that is what it is. I couldn't say that is what it was... that when you have it on...*

B: I never use it...

D: *You never use it at all?*

B: No, I keep it because it was hers. I keep it for myself, but never use it.

D: *Ok, so where do you have it? Do you have it displayed?*

B: No, I have it in the closet.

D: *NO! NO! NO! [Spoken with an Italian accent.]*

[Bianca laughs.]

D: *I hear three "NOs" in a row, I'm sorry, it is just her and she is saying "NO! NO! NO! You're not enjoying it! It needs to be out. You need to see it, you need to enjoy it." I know you don't want to use it and I don't know if you have something that you can display it on. When you see it, when you put your hands on it, when you touch it, you're going to feel her energy and you're going to feel so much better every time you see it, smile, because when it is in the closet, no one gets to enjoy it.*

B: Umm hummm.

D: *So when people come over and they say, "Oh, how beautiful, where did you get that? You can say 'my mama' and it can bring her much more alive. That needs to come out. Ok?*

B: Oh boy.

D: *Sorry. [Laughing.]*

B: That is all right, it doesn't fit on my bed. It's too small.

D: *It's ok. It is just that she wanted that to be said.*

The morning of the reading, my left big toe felt as though it were hurt or injured. I also had the desire to pick at my toe during our reading, which prompted me to ask her about her toes and if she was experiencing any pain. Sure enough, she was.

D: *Who has the, on the left foot, the toe that hurts?*

B: Me.

D: *Ok, because she started telling me that your toe hurts. She is telling me walks would be hard for you. She is telling me you need to get that looked at, but I know they won't do anything for it.*

B: No.

D: *It is weird; she says you need to pay more attention to your foot. Because I am hearing two things, one you need to get it looked at, and two, they are not going to do anything about it, but you need to pay more attention to it. Your toe really hurts. What did you do to it?*

B: I had surgery, an ingrown toenail. But I cannot do anything because I don't have the nail, they have scraped it and this and that, but...

D: *And you have to cut it just right so it doesn't keep growing? Yeah, that is so weird because when you are talking to me, I was am looking at my toe and picking the corner—she is showing me it!*

[Bianca laughs.]

D: *Yes, you need to take care of it, that is what she is saying, pay attention, watch it and don't let it go... Isn't it funny?*

B: It is really funny, yes, it is my left toe.

D: *You say, "What else does she see?" She sees everything. She sees everything that happens to you—your cooking, your computer, your toe, your headaches—everything that happens to you.*

Although this may seem inconsequential to the average person, Bianca's green chair was important to her mother. Apparently, this was where Josephina likes to sit when she was with her.

D: *Something green, I don't know where I am coming up with green, I don't know if it is a chair or a car, but it is green. Hummmmm. Green—what color chair are you sitting in?*

B: It is an orange leather chair.

D: *Right, leather. Hummm. Hummm. Does your daughter have a green chair? Because all of a sudden we were talking about your daughter and I saw green. Green is also for healing too. Is your daughter not feeling...*

B: Yeah, I have a green chair!

D: *You do?*

B: Yeah, I have a green chair in the family room.

D: *Ok, thank you, and do you sit in it?*

B: My husband sits in it more than me.

D: *When he is not sitting in it, then she is.*

B: My mother?

D: *Yes. She just kind of sits and watches everything. So if you are sitting, that chair is at an angle facing something...*

B: It faces the TV.

D: *Yeah. So when you walk by it and no one is there, put a smile on your face. That will make her happy.*

B: Ok.

D: *She likes that green chair because she can see a lot from it.*

B: Yeah. The TV, the backyard, and the kitchen.

Finally, Anna gave Bianca many thanks for holding her hand prior to her crossing over. Bianca's timing was impeccable and the bond they shared endures today. Anna said that she would be there for Bianca when she crosses over.

D: *Anna Anna Anna… Anna wants to talk now, if that is Ok?*

B: Ok.

D: *Unless you have something else from your mom? Anna is very careful with her words. Um, when I first had her down on paper, she was a chatterbox, and I thought, "Ohmigosh, we can't let her in or the two of you are going to talk nonstop and I won't get a word in." That is how… she misses that, she misses conversations with you. You know how you light the candle, she is saying, "Talk to me, talk to me out loud, talk to me in your head. Have those conversations with me, I want to have conversations with you." If something pops into your head, it is Anna saying it to you. Anna says you are funny. Anna has great passion for you. She holds your hand. Did you hold her hand for something? Like when she passed or for something?*

B: How do you know that????! [Bianca says inquisitively.]

D: *Because she is showing… telling me that…*
B: The day before she died…

115

D: *She is thanking you. Because of you holding her hand, it gave her great peace. She knows she was safe to cross over. And she is telling you that she has never stopped holding your hand.*

B: In Italy, she used to call me "Chitta." Chitta in English means "baby." It's a nickname and she called me and said, "Chitta, if you want to see me one more time, it's better you come over because I am very sick." And I went to Italy and the day before she passed away I was there with her.

D: *Ummm humm. She said because you held her hand it made it easier to know when it was time to go and she said she has never let go of your hand, she is always at your side.*

B: Ohmigod. Say hello from me.

D: *Oh, she hears you. She is saying when you cross over, the two of you are going to skip to the other side, holding hands.*

[Bianca laughs again.]

✦   ✦   ✦

Because I try not to criticize others for their beliefs, I ask others not to criticize mine. I believe that a spirit's eyes see what we are not capable of seeing. I believe they view everything in life out of pure love. I do not believe there are malicious spirits. To me, they are lost spirits. People may believe spirits are bad because they feel uncomfortable, uncertain, or unsettled around them. I believe they are a lost spirit trying to get attention so that we know they are around.

I have also learned repeatedly through my readings that spirits will not say something if you are not ready or if you fear hearing from them. It is up to individuals to decide for themselves if talking to a spirit is right or wrong for them. From the example above, Bianca had waited over sixty years to re-connect with her mother. Because she was ready and willing, her loved ones came through vividly.

I have found that a person who usually contacts a medium is someone who needs to contact a deceased loved one. If the individual has not lost a loved one, then why would he or she have interest in a medium or why others do? A skeptic may engage a medium for the pure debate, but in order to get something genuine out of a reading, I believe that a sitter's heart and mind must be truly open with the desire and need for me to process any messages being sent.

I also believe arguing or wanting things done a particular way makes it difficult for a medium to function effectively and may lead to failure. Many skeptics come to a reading with the expectation of what they think they want to hear from a spirit. I have said this before–this is a mistake. Their deceased loved one often has another agenda based on what they believe is important for them to communicate. They must have an open mind or they will likely miss the entire point of the reading.

It also has occurred where I have received little information or none at all. It takes three individuals to make a reading work–the sitter, the spirit, and the medium. If one does not mesh within the trio, then the reading may not work. For example, a spirit may not be comfortable with a particular medium and therefore may not choose to engage. If this is the case, a skeptic may argue that the medium is a fraud. In contrast, a scientist may give the benefit of the doubt and test the medium under a different circumstance.

I may not always know why a reading does not go as planned or does not come easily. Again, my motto has been to trust the spirits because they have never let me down, so why would they start now? Therefore, I believe if words in a reading are not coming through then there must be a higher reason, albeit I may never understand why.

Skeptics typically dispute everything a medium says. For instance, I may tell a skeptic that I see a large dog, like a black lab, next to his loved one. Being skeptic, he would agree that there was a dog, but may discount my accuracy because his loved one owned a black lab mix. By comparison, a scientist may take what was said and try to validate each word. He may confirm the spirit had a black dog in his previous life, and if so, was it a black lab? A scientist dissects the facts to validate *any* level of accuracy.

✦   ✦   ✦

On another note, I have had many individuals question me why I charge for a reading if I have this extraordinary gift. A skeptic would say I am doing this only for the money—to capitalize and take money from grieving people. To them I say it is because it takes time away from my family and the other activities I could be doing. Since readings are time-consuming, I must hire people to assist with my home upkeep (for example, house cleaner, daycare, and gardener) because twenty-four hours is not enough time for me to do this job and manage a household. This path in life is rewarding for both the sitters and me, and it is important for me to continue with this journey.

I stated above that I believe it is my purpose in life is to use my gift to bring humanity compassion and love. I want to touch people physically and spiritually, in order to help bring more public awareness. I want to help those that are grieving. I want to let them know that life is eternal. I want them to have the comfort of knowing their loved ones are fine and continue to exist. I want to give them hope and peace that they will see them again. They need to know their loved ones are with them every day.

I also continue to help in the survival of consciousness research so that science can use the facts from my readings to prove we continue to live after we die. If we are open to it, then we can have a better knowledge and understanding of what will happen to us when we cross over into the afterlife. With this, we can abandon our fears of the unknown.

If we know and believe this information, the question then becomes, "How would we change our lives if we knew our lives never ended?" Dr. Schwartz uses this question in his teachings. He states, "The challenge is to imagine life without any boundaries, between this world and the next." Dr. Schwartz continues, "And that as the caterpillar eventually becomes a butterfly, you too, will in time be able to take flight in ways we cannot yet fathom." [16]

✦   ✦   ✦

Simply put, I believe skeptics base their beliefs out of fear and scientists base their beliefs on facts and truth. Although scientists need concrete evidence in order to prove a medium is talking with a specific spirit, they will believe the spirit exists with the validation of facts given. Through science, the afterlife has been proven to exist. We do not know yet how vast, profound, mysterious, or wondrous it is, but there is proof that we live on and on. Now, if only the skeptics could perceive the truth, they too could be believers.

Just as starlight from distant stars continues forever, the scientists have noted, so does human consciousness. [17]

✦ 9 ✦

<u>Suicide</u>

WHEN A LOVED ONE PASSES BECAUSE OF SUICIDE, I believe everyone around becomes a victim too. No one really wins, not even the deceased. It is a tragic loss that I believe can be prevented with the appropriate care. Often, suicide victims leave their loved ones with more heartache and anguish than was originally present before their passing.

I am also not particularly fond of the word "suicide." By definition, it is an act or an instance of deliberately killing oneself. This is true, in theory, but I believe suicide can better be defined as someone intentionally hurting oneself, which ultimately leads to death. Some may argue it is semantics, but I think of suicide like a disease or illness. It is what kills someone; it is not the act of killing oneself.

Suicide can be simply summed up as an illness of the mind. This illness makes its victims think irrationally. They *think* they want to die because they *think* they are unable to cope with their problems or are mentally incapable of facing daily life. They believe their death would be a better solution to their personal problems rather than wading through them, come what may.

There is also no stereotypical suicide victim. If you read the newspapers, you will see that suicide does not discriminate by race, age, gender, or financial bracket. It can happen to anyone.

Although some victims may be clinically diagnosed as mentally ill, others are not. They can be average, ordinary individuals burdened with intense stress or unbearable emotional pain, which leads them to this irrational space.

Based on my research and experience, an undiagnosed depression is the most common factor leading to suicide. Such despair and misery overpower these victims and cause them to want to end their lives hastily. They may use such tools as firearms, alcohol, lynches, carbon dioxide, or drugs.

Our health care system should give more attention to this devastating illness. If these individuals receive the therapy or treatment they needed to help their minds function properly, then they could potentially avoid the ultimate sacrifice—their life. Therefore, the act of killing oneself should be looked upon as an inquietude, or reckless, accident. If the person were in a clear or peaceful state of mind, then suicide would not prevail.

Studies have shown that many suicide survivors do not ultimately want death. They want assistance in making their pain stop. Many victims seek out medical help prior to their deaths. Since these people cannot make rational choices, they often impetuously succumb to suicide to end their suffering prior to any medical treatment can take affect. Again, these victims should not be labeled as psychotic or insane. They are extremely ill and have, what I consider, a disease. Healthy people do not commit suicide. They face their demons, problems, and challenges head on.

When a suicide victim prepares for death, some choose to write letters while others choose to leave the reason for their death a mystery. I think when letters are written, it is truly their last cry for help. Correspondingly, many make their final arrangements, including a will. I assume that these individuals are diligent in their planning in hopes of lessening the burden on those left behind. Although thoughtful, such acts may prove to be little consolation for their loved ones in the faces of grief and guilt.

✦   ✦   ✦

My father Frank and I are both victims of suicide. I am a survivor of suicide, and my father was the victim of suicide. The survivors of suicide deal with many emotions over the death of suicide. For me, the foremost emotion was anger. I questioned, "How could he have done this? To me? My family?" Some survivors become closer and realize the value of life and each other. Other survivors blame one another hoping to alleviate the guilt they have for being part of the cause.

Unforgettable actions or unforgivable words may be exchanged between loved ones who are left to pick up the pieces. This grief can lead to more pain and frustration. I had to witness devastating actions from loved ones, including my father. They may be unforgettable, but with time, they became forgivable. I learned that forgiveness is one of life's greatest gifts, but one of the hardest lessons to grasp. When we forgive someone or something, we release our own pain.

To release my pain, I faced my feelings through journaling. What I mean by journaling is that I wrote letters or notes to my father and loved ones. Not literally, I did not send them, but I wrote them and kept them for my own sake.

Survivors may need to let out their anger, speak from their heart, say what should have been said, release their guilt, say I am sorry, or write anything else that may be directed at their loved one. Once these honest feelings are surrendered in their journaling, then they can start to heal and perhaps be inspired to write their deceased loved one a love letter. This exercise allows a person to say the last words that were never said.

When journaling, survivors should realize their words are being released to their loved one. Based on prior chapters, one should know that spirits hear such words and thoughts and can help take the pain away. In return for the pain they caused, the spirits want to help heal. Therefore, if survivors keep their feelings within, then they are not opening themselves to the healing process.

Such feelings may emerge another time in another way. Some survivors get depressed, sick, or become unable deal with their own life challenges. This may surface months, or even years, later. That is why it is common for a suicide to cause depression in others coping with the loss of a loved one. I was told this was normal when grieving for someone who has committed suicide. I was completely devastated, and then depressed, because I had so many questions that were unanswered initially.

✛　　✛　　✛

When my father was alive, he became a person that I did not know. Unfortunately, I did not grasp what was happening. He was suffering as a victim of an undiagnosed depression. It took my family and me many years to reach this conclusion. He was dealing with chronic depression, which ultimately led to hopelessness and desperation. Similar to someone dying from an incurable cancer, he was slowly dying inside.

I now look at my father's death with mixed emotion. On one hand, his death was ultimately a tragedy because he was unable to seek the proper medical care or family help that may have changed his outcome. On the other hand, he no longer had to suffer and face the agonizing days he was experiencing. He joined his wife and entered the afterlife.

As a medium, I confidently can clear a myth that so many people struggle to understand. Many believe if a person commits suicide, he or she will not go to heaven and join the afterlife. This is absolutely untrue! As noted in prior chapters, I hear, see, feel, and speak to my father whenever I wish. I am blessed to be a medium and have this connection with him. I have also talked with other spirits that crossed over as a result of suicide. Does anyone with cancer, heart disease, or any other ailment get punished for the way they passed? If not, then why should those with an illness I call suicide be punished?

Having said the above, suicide should never be viewed as a last resort or the only solution. In fact, it should not be considered at all. My father told me that he experienced his own healing on the other side with the assistance of his guides and angels. He had to grow and accept his issues in order to move through them and past them. It saddens me that he felt suicide was the only remedy for his earthly mind and body. I truly believe that if he had endured through his pain and encountered such healing while on earth, he would physically be with me today.

Suicide victims become a true victim after they cross over and are able to see their life for what it truly was or could have been. They may realize that they cut their life short and failed to complete their life's journey. At that point, they may wish that they did not stop living on earth because they finally can appreciate the value of their life.

Suicide victims are just like other spirits. They continue to exist in the afterlife. They are happy and healthy. They are with you throughout your days. I once again have the father I used to love and know before his illness. I forgave him for everything he did. We now share a new life together. It is a completely new beginning for both of us, but I must say, I wish it were here on earth.

Before, I could never understand why people would selfishly commit suicide and bring so much grief to their families and friends. I now understand it is more than just a selfish act.

When anyone asks me how my father passed, I do not use the harsh word "suicide." Instead, I tell them he died in an unfortunate accident. If you have lost a loved one to suicide, please see it as a mindless accidental death, not a willful death. Please believe your loved one is now a living soul. Then the blessing is twofold: their pain and suffering has ended and they finally feel the peace, happiness, and security they so desperately desired in this life.

✟   ✟   ✟

<u>DELORES</u> AND <u>FRANK</u> <u>PUEHRINGER</u>

*(February 9, 1931 to December 7, 1984 and
December 18, 1928 to May 17, 1987, respectively)*

✦ 10 ✦

<u>Connected</u>

On February 4, 2002, I was eight months pregnant and on bed rest. While watching the evening news, the anchors led with a story of a fatal car accident. It involved four teenage boys from two local high schools. The accident occurred the prior evening.

Since my oldest son attended one of the schools, I realized immediately that I might know all of the boys involved. I prayed I did not. I sat with a pit in my stomach anxiously listening. When they flashed pictures on the screen, I said to myself, "Dear God!" It was the son of a family we knew well.

I wondered why we had not heard about this earlier. The boy's name was Chase. Chase and his older brother were the same ages as my two oldest children. Since we grew up in the same neighborhood, they all knew each other well.

The news then said that two of the four teens passed away. I questioned myself, "Did Chase pass? Did they show his picture because he passed or because he was in the car accident? Why did they only show two boys and not all four?" Although I had limited information, I needed to inform my children. I called them into the room and told them the devastating news. They immediately made calls to their friends and

127

found out that Chase was one of the survivors. However, he was in extremely critical condition.

✦   ✦   ✦

Three weeks later, my youngest daughter was born. She arrived five weeks early. Because her lungs were underdeveloped, she was having difficulty breathing on her own. She was placed in the neonatal intensive care unit. My husband and I were a complete mess. Was I going to lose my daughter? Although she was my fourth child, she was my husband's first. I prayed, "This can't be happening to us."

As I entered the neonatal unit, there was a picture of a boy, which looked just like Chase, taped to the window facing the unit. The boy's name was Dustin. Next to the picture was the article about the car accident, which occurred about four weeks prior. I was unable to read the article because of the way it hung in the window.

Every time I saw the picture, I could not help but wonder, "Why was this boy's picture on the window? Was he alive? Had he passed?" I then thought to myself, "Perhaps the picture was placed there for prayers?"

I passed this window several times per day for almost an entire week. I was drawn to look at Dustin and wondered each time if he were alive. For some reason, I never asked the nurses about Dustin's picture, nor found out any of the answers to my questions while my daughter was there. I must have been focused on her and the other babies in that unit. Shortly thereafter, we were blessed to go home with a healthy baby girl.

I soon learned that Chase's picture was not supposed to be on the news.

It should have been his close friend Dustin's picture. Because Chase and Dustin looked so much alike, their photos were reversed. The news that night showed pictures of the two boys that died the night before. Their names were Dustin and Andrew. Tragically, they were both only fifteen years old. Dustin's older brother Cameron, and Chase, were the two survivors.

✦   ✦   ✦

About six months later, Andrew's mother Katie requested a reading with me. Katie's primary concern was if her son died alone. Andrew came through immediately. He said that he liked the board that was placed next to his bed. I told her that the board I was seeing had lots of writing on it.

Katie explained that it was a memorial board with messages from all of his friends. She told me that Andrew was a popular kid in high school and that many peers gravitated toward him.

Andrew continued and showed me a shoe. I could feel that he was very upset about this shoe. Katie did not know what he was referencing. This comment made no sense to her. She told me that she received all of his items from the accident. Even so, I told her that he was persistent in showing me the shoe and was still anxious and upset over it. Katie made a note to research it, and we continued.

Andrew then told me that he tried to hang on for her sake. He wanted to wait for her before he passed, but a familiar face came to him. It was his grandmother, Katie's mother, who had already passed and was there to help him. Andrew said that he was not afraid and felt safe. He said he continued to try to hang on, but it was too hard. He said that he had to let go and was sorry. He said that his grandmother took his hand and helped him cross over.

Katie was at peace knowing Andrew was not alone when he died. We ended our reading with Andrew telling his mother to sit in a green chair at their home. He said that in that chair she would be able to feel his energy and know that he is still around. Andrew also asked his mother to talk to him because he could hear her.

Although the reading was over that day, Katie and I became friends. On the one-year anniversary of Andrew's passing, Katie, along with some of the other boys' families, visited the accident site for a memorial. Prior to going, she read the notes from our reading. The missing shoe still puzzled her.

While they were at the site, Chase found the shoe Andrew spoke about in our reading. Katie was amazed and grateful. Because Chase had bigger feet, he would pass his shoes onto Andrew. Chase immediately recognized it at the site and brought it to her. Andrew was wearing Chase's old shoes in the accident. Finding this shoe gave Katie another confirmation that it was Andrew talking during our session. From that day on, Katie told me that Andrew continually showed her signs to let her know that he exists in her everyday life.

✦   ✦   ✦

In October 2002, Dustin's parents asked me for a reading as well. I could tell during our initial introduction that his father was somewhat skeptical. He told me repeatedly that he wanted to hear certain words in order to make him a believer. I understood someone needing verification to know if it was a loved one, but to come with explicit expectations was a recipe for disappointment. On the other hand, Dustin's mother

Helene was anxious to hear from her son. She was ready to receive anything that would come though.

Thankfully, Dustin joined us and provided many details that day. I felt the most important part of our reading was when he asked that each of his brothers have something special of his. He asked his parents to give one brother his shell necklace and his other brother his watch. Helene was amazed. She told me that they had already given Dustin's brothers these items.

Before leaving, Dustin told his mother that she would smell an unusual scent, like a flower, at peculiar times. He said that when she experienced these scents, she should think of him and know that he was around.

Two weeks later, Helene was in her car on her way to a bereavement class. A strong smell of coconut was present. She took four deep breaths and smelled it each time. After the fourth, the smell disappeared. Dustin loved this tropical scent. He had coconut lotion and enjoyed virgin piña coladas. Helene told me that this was confirmation from her son that everything that was said in the reading was from him.

✦　　✦　　✦

A few weeks later, a nurse from the neonatal intensive care unit that cared for my daughter contacted me for a reading. Dustin's mother, Helene, referred her to me. The pieces to the puzzle seemed to fall together when we spoke. Helene was also a nurse who worked at the neonatal unit. I never met her there because she was on bereavement leave. That was why her son's picture was posted on the window.

Helene's friend, I will call her Pam, contacted me because she had lost her husband recently. Pam was looking for closure. We agreed to meet at her home for the reading. As she opened the door to greet me, we both recognized one another immediately. Pam was the head nurse that oversaw my daughter and guided the other nurses. Now it was my turn to help her.

I believe it is a blessing when things work out this way. People never know when they receive help if they will ever be given the chance to reciprocate. This reading lasted for four hours, much longer than a typical reading. Because her husband died tragically, they were able to say their good-byes and ultimately give each other permission to move forward.

In the end, we both had an enormous amount of gratitude toward one another. She gave me one of my most cherished gifts, a healthy baby girl to take home, and I gave her peace and comfort knowing her husband would watch over her.

✦ ✦ ✦

In May 2003, about fifteen months since the passing of Dustin and Andrew, I was asked by Helene for a second reading. This time, Helene said that she would be alone. She told me that her husband had emotionally and mentally separated from her after their son's death. As a result, she was often depressed.

Before we started the reading, Helene shared with me that Dustin had come to her recently on Mother's Day. She showed me a beautiful antique clock that hung on her hallway wall. She told me that it was very old and did not work. However, on Mother's Day, it began to keep time, but then stopped again. The time the clock stopped was the same hour of Dustin's death. These three facts—the clock working, on Mother's Day, and stopping at the same hour—gave her confirmation it was her son wishing her a Happy Mother's Day. I agreed that it must have been Dustin. He could not have given her any better gift.

During our reading, Dustin came through strong. He was specific and told her the separation with his father was not caused by his death. He repeatedly stated it would have happened anyway. He gave his mother permission to be happy and urged her to engage in living a full life. She no longer needed to take on the negative energy of his father.

During our reading, we digressed for a while. I mentioned to Helene that I had met her co-worker Pam. I told her that I did not realize that she worked at the neonatal intensive care unit until I met Pam. She asked me when my daughter was born. I told her on February 25, 2002. I explained that she was in this unit because she had complications with her under-developed lungs. I told her I saw her son's picture there every day yet never knew why it was posted.

I said to her, "You must have been on leave during this time—that is why we never saw one another or met." She disagreed and continued, "I was the nurse that took care of your daughter." She then described the exact location of where her crib was in the neonatal nursery. My daughter was the first baby assigned to her after her leave of absence. Pam assigned her my daughter because she felt that she was the least risky, making her one of the easier babies to care for. I was stunned and could not believe that we had not made this connection earlier. At the time, because both of us were experiencing such devastating situations, we were unable to remember one another. I thought to myself, "Amazing, I am helping her now, and she has already helped me."

After this revelation, Dustin and Andrew both joined in. Their presence was incredibly strong to me. I felt like I wanted to cry, but did not know why yet. Both of the boys wanted to speak directly to me, not just through me. I was confused. Why did they want to talk to me? It soon made perfect sense.

The boys told me they watched over my daughter and helped her survive in the neonatal intensive care unit. They said, "If we didn't help your daughter live and she died, then we knew you couldn't help our families." I was now sobbing and was stunned.

These two boys gave me a gift of a lifetime, my beautiful healthy daughter—wow! In my medium experience, I do not believe I had ever been so overwhelmed. First, Helene helped my daughter, and now, they too! When I saw Dustin's picture in the window and wondered if he were alive, I was feeling his energy. He was there. He was alive, just in the afterlife. This was when I realized an amazing connection.

We are all connected, the spirits and us. We are like a complete circle. We continuously go around and have no end. We guide and help one another. Whether it is a spirit or one person helping another, we are all one. We may not even realize that we are giving or receiving assistance. It just happens. It is what is meant to be. There are no coincidences. I firmly believe that it is more than that.

When I spoke with the mothers of Andrew or Dustin, I always wondered what it would be like to lose a child. It was a heartache that I never wanted to experience. Moreover, Andrew and Dustin were right. If I had lost my daughter while she struggled as a preemie, I would not have had the strength to help their parents or others.

I will forever be grateful to Andrew and Dustin. I send them both peace and love. To their mothers, I will be their friend forever. I will continue to watch them on their life journeys, making sure they are aware of all of their sons' signs. To the two survivors of the accident, Chase and Cameron, may you know that your brother and best friend have never left your side.

It took a complete year for this circle of events to take place. Once we reached the end, the circle was complete. We were all able to witness how connected we truly were with one another and our loved ones who had passed. When someone says it is a small world, it is really smaller than you think. One may never know the importance of the next person they meet. In a time of need, the right person will appear to offer you guidance, support, and comfort. This is not a coincidence; it is just what is meant to be.

I love wearing necklaces with circles. To me, the circle represents life never-ending. We begin in this world and continue in the afterlife, never breaking the connection between both worlds. We all live, from one life to the next, continuously. May we all embrace the connection between both of these remarkable, intriguing, and beautiful worlds.

Dustin James Carroll and Andrew Scott Stevenson
(April 16, 1986 to February 3, 2002 and
March 7, 1987 to February 3, 2002, respectively)

Everything, including our consciousness, is made up of energy, and energy never dies. It only changes form. Everything carries the vibration of life for us to honor. Those who have crossed over have become our greatest teachers in our understanding of the circle of life. It is our responsibility to listen to them. It is our responsibility to share this information with others for it is in our sharing that healing takes place.

-Karyl O'Leary

Personal Validations and Photos

"Every meeting and sharing of persons is an exchange of gifts. My gift is me, your gift is you. We are gifts to each other."

~Author Unknown

In the following pages, you will learn first-hand about many living souls that have re-connected with their loved ones by using me as their voice. It was an honor to meet them because they all left a unique imprint on my heart. I hope that you enjoy reading their stories and meeting them too. They are in no particular order.

I sincerely wish you peace and happiness on your own journey. More importantly, I hope that your loved ones, who have crossed over, will lovingly remind you that they are always by your side even though you cannot see them. I can only hope that after reading my book and these personal validations, you will open your heart and soul and *Believe Beyond Seeing.*

~Debra Martin
Laboratory Research Medium
VERITAS Research Program, University of Arizona
Lab Certified Medium
Forever Family Foundation, Inc.
www.goldenmiracles.com

✦   ✦   ✦

Derrace Ray Hoey

(November 24, 1947 to December 25, 2002)
Gilbert, Arizona

138

My brother Derrace and I experienced an unfortunate alienation shortly before his death. After a very close lifetime relationship, this made his passing a doubly hurtful loss for me. This hurt was eased through my reading with Debbie who relayed message after remarkable message, the majority of which were known only to my brother and me. The most comforting communication was the affirmation of a dream in which my brother came to me in a most vivid way. I awoke in tears from this dream because the brotherly love we shared was reaffirmed. Derrace communicated to Debbie that he had visited me in a dream. I then put her to a test. I asked if he could describe the setting of the dream. Debbie immediately described a large shade tree in a green meadow with a body of water in the background—exactly right!

My father John also made an appearance. A lifelong chain smoker of cigarettes, he presented himself to Debbie as "completely surrounded by smoke." He then solved a household mystery. Debbie relayed that dad was "smiling," and said that I had "smelled his smoke." My wife Beckie's jaw dropped at this. Several times, I had accused her of sneaking a cigarette when I detected the distinct traces of smoke in the house. Having quit smoking years before, she was very happy to say, "I told you so" about her vehement denials.

Debbie left no doubt that our loved ones never truly leave us. The confirmation I received were numerous, specific, and in many cases, known only to my deceased loved ones and me. We do continue to exist beyond this plane and Debbie's gift would convince even the strongest skeptic. Thanks again, Debbie.

~Don Hoey,
brother of Derrace Hoey

<u>JOHN H. PETERS, III</u>

(July 6, 1947 to April 6, 2006)
Scottsdale, Arizona

I spoke with Debra about my husband, John, and his perceived reluctance
to let go of his earthly body to allow his beautiful and loving spirit to
soar and once again be reunited with a higher power. John and I shared
a soul-mate love beginning with our very first encounter some forty-
two years ago. His devastating illness (Creutzfeldt-Jacob) turned our

lives upside down. I had lovingly given him permission to transition; however, I sensed hesitation.

Debra was aware that John and his father had a rather turbulent relationship most of their lives. John's father died on Thanksgiving Day 2003, leaving John challenged with some unresolved issues. I mentioned to Debra that I had a picture of our immediate family hanging in his room at the hospice inpatient unit. That was when Debra said John's mother was coming through to her. John's mother showed Debra that I had a picture of John with his parents sitting on a table in my home. I shared with Debra that I was thinking about taking this picture of John with his parents when he was six or seven years old to the inpatient unit. Debra then heard that I needed to find a picture of just John and his mother. The picture could not have his father in it. In fact, Debra stated that I would find such a picture behind the picture of all three of them. Debra stated John's mother wanted him to know she was with him. So if John saw this picture he would be comforted knowing she was by his side now and ready to take his hand when he was crossed over.

Without hesitation, I immediately took the picture frame apart and there it was—a beautiful picture of John and his mother. Again, John appeared to be six or seven years old. That same day I took the picture to the hospice unit and placed it in plain view on his nightstand. It was obvious to me that John recognized his mother. The picture brought him a great deal of peace.

On April 6, 2006, John was joyfully reunited with his family and friends and was lovingly embraced in the arms of God. I also know that he will always be my Guardian Angel. I tell him every day how blessed I was to have found him at such a young age. He was a special husband, wonderful father, adoring grandfather, and terrific friend to many, including me. I find great comfort in knowing beyond a shadow of a doubt that he will live in my heart and walk by my side through the rest of my journey here on earth.

Debra Martin, I am eternally grateful to you for your love and insight. Most of all, I am grateful that you have the courage to honor and share your God-given gift with others. Bless you, my friend.

~Judy Peters,
wife of John H. Peters, III

Josephine Mae Catalano

(June 1, 1932 to November 2, 2004)
Phoenix, Arizona.

I was married to Mae Catalano on April 26, 1959, and she was "the love of my life." My reading with Debbie was very special because I was able to connect with her again and feel so close to her. Mae told me, through Debbie, to quit being so lazy and slice some fruit. She was telling me that I needed to eat more fruit for breakfast. I knew without a doubt that it was Mae because she used to slice me fruit every morning.

~Charlie Catalano,
Mae's husband
(1925 to January 19, 2006)

143

ELIOT RUSSELL FOWLE

(December 6, 1910 to June 12, 1990)
Nahant, Massachusetts

My dad was my best buddy when I was growing up. When he was not at work, I was his shadow. He had a passion for adventure, told great stories, and loved to make people smile. My dad taught me how to fish, garden, beach comb, cook, play cribbage, backgammon, and tell good jokes. His passing left me with a devastating void in my heart. I long to call him and share my experiences with him or ask him questions as I was so used to doing when I moved away from home.

When I learned that Debbie was a medium, I told her of my wish to re-connect with my dad. There have been many signs throughout the years I have experienced, signs that he was with me. Were they real, or was it wishful thinking? Debbie and I made plans to spend some time together while our husbands attended a conference. One spring day in 2006, I flew from Boston to Scottsdale full of excitement to meet Debbie for the first time. It turned out to be an amazing day. I would like to share a few of our magical moments so you will have comfort knowing that true love *IS* forever!

When we met, Debbie started out by saying that my dad wanted me to know that he was with me. We talked about the signs I witnessed. They included: the appearance of a hawk, the quick shadow I saw over my right shoulder, the chill I felt, the butterflies in my chest, the warmth on my right shoulder, etc. These were all the treasures I found when I opened my mind to them. While she talked to me, she turned her head to the right a bit and gave me the mischievous eye my dad was famous for. She said things in his words, for example, she said, "I see cottage cheese." This made sense to me because my dad loved to make a special dip for crackers with cottage cheese.

She described my guardian angel to me and said she also saw another woman next to me with my dad. I thought it was his mom, but she said, "No, I see a sister." I always wanted to, but never got to meet my aunt. I sent her pictures and letters when I was a little girl. Shocked, I exclaimed Aunt Dorothy?!" Debbie then broke down and cried.

She said in Dottie's words, "You remember me?!" What an incredible moment knowing that she was with me too!

Debbie proceeded to tell me that my dad was concerned with the inner conflict that I was experiencing. She said that I needed to know that he wants me to live my life with LOVE and JOY. I am telling you this part because it is the major theme for the day, and will be for the rest of my life. Throughout our many conversations, the room got very cold, goose bumps came and went, and I had that fluttering feeling in my chest again. It was all good.

We then went out for lunch and had a lovely time. During lunch, Debbie stated that she saw a whimsical heart, not colored in. The waiter delivered our bill with fortune cookies. My fortune read, "Absence makes the heart grow fonder." I said to Debbie, "What does that mean?" We pondered this, and then I excused myself to the restroom. I returned to find Debbie laughing. She said, "your dad is so funny..." and told me that she found herself staring at a woman's chest realizing that it was her heart necklace that caught her (or my dad's) attention, not her bosom. She wondered, "Why?" My dad then announced to her, "It is all about the heart, and you will see many hearts today."

After lunch, we went shopping. At the first store, I picked up a box without knowing what it was. I turned it over and found a decal of rhinestones in the shape of a heart. Wow! I then picked up a lovely ceramic wall hanging that had a heart decorating the top. I turned it over and written on the back was "May your life be full of LOVE and JOY." I then discovered heart-shaped earrings with roses on them with French lettering– *Poudre de Riz*. I remembered that my dad used call me "ma petite riz plen de pou!" More goose bumps followed!

As the day went on, we saw hearts everywhere! On our walk back home, Debbie stopped at a home furnishing shop and said, "I do not know why, but we need to go in here, there was something on the counter for you."

We went to the check out counter and there were silver boxes in the shape of fortune cookies. I picked one up while Debbie wondered out loud, "What do you think is inside?" I said, "A heart, of course!" I opened it, and there inside was a beautiful mother of pearl, shell heart! I was overwhelmed, speechless, and shocked! Debbie broke down and cried from all of the love that my dad was showing me. We opened all of the other boxes to find out that this was the only box with a heart inside.

I do not think the signs could have been any clearer that day. I no longer feel lonely. As long as I open my heart and take the time to follow it, this intense love will guide me the right direction. This knowledge comforts me and will do so for the rest of my life. My wish for you is that you are able to listen to your heart and find the same comfort. May your life be full of LOVE and JOY too. Best wishes from the bottom of my heart.

~Sally Russell Zagnoli,
daughter of Eliot Russell Fowle

NEIL JOSEPH FEOLA, JR.

(June 10, 1955 to April 16, 2005)
Scottsdale, Arizona

During my reading with Debbie, Neil's personality showed through. There was no doubt in my mind that he was there. It was important to me during the reading to ask for Neil's forgiveness. I had always promised that I would never, ever put him in a nursing home. The amount of guilt I was going through was unbearable. The most important thing that came through during our reading was when Neil said the following: "You should never say 'never.' We did not understand what we were going to be up against. Learn from this and do not ever use the word 'never.'"

Another quote Neil said through the years was "Huntington's [Disease] saved my life. I would have died earlier from drinking, smoking, and over- work if I had not contracted HD [Huntington's Disease]. I realized what was important to me and made it my priority in life. I was happier in the last eight years than ever before."

After my reading with Debbie, I now know that Neil is with me in every aspect of my life. He may be gone physically, but I feel him every single moment. I have learned to slow myself down and open my heart and soul. He is always there showing me the way and loving me.

The picture above was taken shortly after he had been diagnosed with Huntington's Disease. Neil loved the water. Despite the fact that he had just received such devastating news, he looked so happy and relaxed.

~Becky Feola,
Neil's wife

Donna Mae Turing

(August 1, 1930 to October 13, 1999)
Fargo, North Dakota

When I received a Debra Martin reading as a Christmas gift from my brother-in-law and sister-in-law, I was excited to learn what occurred during a reading. My sister-in-law shared with me her experiences with readings, but I had yet to fully "get it." How did it work? What should I expect? How could I be sure my loved one–my mother–would communicate with me through a medium? I was open, but I have to admit, I was skeptical.

I wanted to reach my mother, who passed away in 1999 after battling lung cancer for over three years. Since that time, I carried a burden of knowing I had not been able to accept her imminent death, and as a result, was not able to talk to her about dying. I always believed she wanted and needed to talk about it, and I let her down. So when the time came for my reading, I was interested, but nervous and anxious.

After the reading began, I quickly learned what a warm and genuine person Debra was. She immediately made me feel comfortable. As she described various words, actions, and visuals, memory after memory surfaced. Within a short period of time, I had no doubt my mother was communicating with me through Debra. I was laughing; I was in tears; it was an emotional roller- coaster throughout the reading.

I try now to think of a word to describe how I felt as the conversation ended. Maybe the right word is "awakened"–awakened to the belief that losing a loved one does not mean cutting off communication. I felt a sense of awe in the reality of what had happened. I warmly reflect on the conversation, which re-established the link I had felt was not available to me after my mother's death. I continue to re-run the reading in my head, and find myself smiling as I remember the messages shared.

~Deb O'Leary,
daughter of Donna Turing

THOMAS PETER OCASIO
(July 18, 1939 to July 8, 2005)
New York

I lost my dad to suicide on July 8, 2005. As you would expect, I was in shock and disbelief. I knew for the prior six months that he was depressed. I was blessed that I was able to see him in May 2005 because my dad lived in New York and I lived in Phoenix, Arizona. While my dad was with me, I tried to talk to him about his depression. I let him know that I had a bout with depression once, but I went to a doctor and anti-depressants were prescribed. I got better after that. I told him that I would help him in any way and that things would be ok.

My session with Debbie occurred three months after my father had passed. It was a life-saver for me. You see, I never met Debbie in person. We just talked on the phone. I knew my father was with us within the first two minutes of our conversation. My dad had a very bad habit of pacing—it would just drive one up the wall. When talking with Debbie, she mentioned that she just had this overwhelming need to pace. From there, our time together on the phone continued to go well. I had many questions that I wanted to ask, and she was able to get the answers for me. Our phone session allowed me to be at total ease. I could cry, laugh, or just make funny faces when she would tell me things. I could just be me.

I was shocked or surprised—and happy—when I asked about a name of an individual, she accurately told me about that person. She told me how my father felt about them and what I needed to know. I am now at peace with my dad's death. Debbie allowed me to have one last conversation with him. I know with all of my heart and soul that when I was talking with Debbie that my dad was with us. Thank you, Debbie.

-Josephine Johnson,
daughter of Thomas Ocasio

KENNETH GENE KNECHT

(June 27, 1961 to November 22, 2001)
Gardner, North Dakota

Some things come into our lives and are quickly gone, like a spectacular sunset or a radiant rainbow. Some things, like the beautiful bird I refer to as "My Raven" has stayed near since the devastating loss of my son. It has given me a much deeper understanding of what is significant in this life and a feeling of peace about the hereafter. This wonderful sign from my son touches my soul and gives me strength. When I hear the raven's call, it brings happiness to my heart, and my life will never be the same.

The first thing Debra asked when she arrived at our home for our reading was "Where is the bird?" This question was written on a note pad she was carrying. Debra explained that she was told by Ken that when she came into our home she would see a bird because that is his sign to let me know he is always with me. Upon entering our foyer is a magnificent, life-size bronze raven. Our home is filled with many sculptures and pictures of this spiritual bird, gentle reminders that the love my son and I share will go on forever. Those four words from Debra were absolute confirmation that the information she gave came directly from my son. There were numerous amazing validations during our reading with Debra. She is a brilliant medium who truly cares about those with whom she shares her gift. Communicating with my son through Debra was an experience I will always treasure.

~Karyl O'Leary,
mother of Kenneth Knecht

<u>SEAN MARC GERBER</u>

(August 27, 1968 to September 6, 1996)
Anaheim, California

I was moving books to new shelves we just had built and a card fell out of one of them. It was a Father's Day card from 1996 from our son Sean to his dad three months before Sean died. That night I had a dream about him, which I rarely do. The next morning when I went into the kitchen, there was a piece of paper on the floor. When I picked it up it had Debbie's name and phone number on it. My first thought was that Sean wanted to contact me. But I did not get around to e-mailing her that day.

About one week later, I got a catalog in the mail and when I finished reading it I noticed that it had been sent to Sean at our address. However, he had not lived with us at this address, so why did it arrive here? I thought he must really need to talk, so I e-mailed Debbie immediately.

When she called back, she told me that Sean really needed to talk to his sister Kim, but it was too noisy at her house. Through Debbie, Sean told me that there would be a big change in Kim's life and it was a good one. He said that he was there to help her and her husband, Mark. He also said that a prior business relationship, which Mark was in the process of ending, was not a good one and that it was best that it ended. Debra told me that Sean wanted me to stop worrying and trust that they were going to be fine. Debra's reading gave me validation that it was my son Sean saying, "Stop worrying mom!" At the time, I relayed his message to Kim. We soon learned his words were right on because it turned out to be a great career move for Mark.

~Mel Gerber,
mother of Sean Gerber

MARK ARNOLD

(April 7, 1957 to October 9, 2004)
Cave Creek, Arizona

Mark's personality came through so clearly, even before I hired Debbie to do my reading! She and I were having our first phone conversation about setting up an appointment, and there he was, already butting into our conversation! Anyone that has spent time around Mark knows he was never one to sit by and let things happen around him. He was always right there in the middle of things *making* them happen! That was so typical of him, and I knew at that point that he was already there waiting (very anxiously) to talk to me. There were also so many very specific things that were said to me during the reading that only he could have known. There is no way in the world that Debbie, or anyone else, could have ever guessed the personal things that came through in my reading. I know without any doubt that Mark was speaking to me that day, and he is still here with us.

-Jamie Amborn,
Mark's friend

NICHOLAS E. WILSON
(January 2, 1984 to March 11, 2005)
Glendale, Arizona

I think the thing that made me a true believer was when he was talking to me and he told you we were there (at your house, the semi-truck thing… spooky). He talked non-stop (as he always did when he was excited) and he answered my questions *before* I asked them. The things that stand out to me as validations include: his knowing where we placed his pictures in the house, he liking things we had done at his funeral, and telling Rebecca what to wear when she was down–his favorite plaid shirt!!!! He also told us *how* he died and that he felt NO PAIN!!!! It was as if we were all together. Your gift is a true gift, and I appreciate the feeling of peace you have given Rebecca and me.

~Debbie Newhouse,
mother of Nicholas Wilson

MERALD OSCAR PETERSON

(August 17, 1930 to September 23, 2002)
Gilbert, Arizona

I have not been able to feel dad's presence like before and have been missing him a lot. Last Friday was the third anniversary of his death. I decided to substitute teach for our music teacher. The teacher had left "game day" instructions for me as well as some CD's to choose from to play a game called "freeze dance". The CD on top was the one I chose and the first track happened to be my dad's favorite song. I spent the morning dancing away to dad's favorite band and song. It was not until after lunch that I remembered what anniversary the day was!!! What a blessing God and dad gave me that day; I had a wonderful time listening to his music and playing with kids. Thanks for opening my eyes to the signs that he is still around me. I miss him so much.

~Beth Dickson,
daughter of Merald Peterson

Don and Carole

CAROLE MARIE HEYEN
(January 14, 1934 to 1994)
Glendale, Wisconsin

Carole told Debbie to have me make Todd's favorite cookie for Christmas. I was shocked when she specifically mentioned the kind of cookie—peanut butter kiss cookies. I was so stunned I did not know what to say. This confirmed for me that Carole is watching over us.

~Mary Jo Heyen,
daughter-in-law of Carole Marie Heyen

Sharon Schlink Clouse

(May 31, 1939 to April 1, 1999)
Mesa, Arizona

Debbie studied the brooch on my sweater. She asked what it was, exactly, because my mom was telling her that there was something significant about it. "Is it a flower?" she inquired. I replied that it was, and she asked me if there was something special about flowers with my mom. I tried to think about my mom and flowers, but she was never a big 'flower person', so I told Debbie that I could not make any sort of connection between the two.

Debbie continued, "No, it is not flowers, but one flower in particular. You have a flower hidden somewhere because you are afraid something will happen to it. I see it put away in some sort of dark cabinet where it can be kept safe. Your mom knows this flower is very special to you and that you are worried your boys might harm it." The tears started flowing as I remembered the flower that I gingerly tucked in the back of an armoire.

"Now I remember," I whispered. "One of my mother's friends dried the yellow roses from the spray that adorned my mother's casket. She gave one to each of us girls. I used to keep mine out on a shelf next to a picture of my mom as a small reminder, but several years ago, I put it safely in a cabinet because I was afraid a stray ball or careless boy of mine would accidentally harm it." That is when I knew—I was sitting there, having lunch with my friend Debbie and my mom, who died five years earlier.

~Terry Thomas,
daughter of Sharon Clouse

SARAH MELISSA SAPLIS

(August 12, 1983 to June 9, 2003)
Scottsdale, Arizona

My experience with Debbie Martin is one that I can hardly put into words. The enlightenment and peace that I obtained after meeting with her is something for which I am truly grateful. I now hold a strong belief that my beloved sister, Sarah, is still around, and our bond is everlasting. One of my favorite memories actually occurred following my phone reading with Debbie. She immediately called me back with a sense of urgency to express Sarah's pain and sympathy for me having my eyebrows waxed or plucked. In fact, two days earlier, I had my eyebrows waxed for the first time in preparation for my Senior Prom. Just thinking about it brings a smile to my face. I want to thank

Debbie, from the bottom of my heart, for giving me the chance to share such a wonderful experience. She put my mind at ease and my heart at rest.

~Jennifer Saplis,
sister of Sarah Saplis

I wanted you to know what the reading with Debbie and my daughter has meant to me as well as her. We had readings together previously as a family with psychics, but it was especially important for my daughter Jenny to have one by herself. Although Jenny's experience with Debbie was extremely personal and rewarding, Debbie also shared with her some messages to pass along to me that deeply touched and amazed me. Debbie said, "Your mom is having an extremely difficult time handling Sarah's death," which most anyone would imagine. What really struck me was when Debbie said, "She is referring to your mom as 'Mama' instead of 'Mom'." This was something I was especially fond of. I hear her calling me Mama in my head all of the time since she has been gone. Even though Sarah was a beautiful, mature nineteen-year-old young woman, she usually called me Mama. I believed this was to reassure me that even though we were like best friends, she was still, and will always be, my little girl.

Debbie also said that Sarah's grandmother was with her and still talked in a funny way that tickled everyone. It was a perfect description of my mom. Debbie suggested that it was her paternal grandmother with Sarah, but she had a very different personality. Even so, there was an incredible amount of accurate information in our readings. I could go on and on.

Debbie asked if Sarah had any neck problems because of the pain that Debbie experienced in her own neck at the time. This was not something that we identified as an issue during Sarah's life. Sarah had died of massive head trauma, just as Debbie stated in an earlier reading. Eight months after the reading at the criminal trial, we were shocked and horrified to see crime scene photos of Sarah with a broken neck. Imagine trying to face each day with such horrific images of your precious child, sibling, or loved one in your mind. There are no words expressive enough to describe the pain, the loss, and the hopelessness.

Thank you, Debbie, for bringing into our lives some sense of peace and hope that has been difficult to find even with our faith in God. We need all of the reassurance we can get to help us believe that Sarah is truly okay and hopefully at peace.

Debbie, I thank you for remembering Sarah and Jenny. There is so much I would like to share with you about Sarah—it helps me keep her alive by doing so. I am hoping you already have a sense of her and her personality and will be able to verify that information through future readings.

~Connie Saplis,
mother of Sarah Saplis

Marcia Gold painted the above artwork.
According to Caron, she submitted this picture because it is what her
mother would have preferred versus a photograph of herself.

Marcia Mazur Gold

(September 1, 1935 to May 12, 2004)
Sedona, Arizona

During my reading with Debbie, I asked my mom, through her, what I should do about Suki. And Debbie replied, "Do you mean the cat who is dying?" Without any hints or clues, she knew the Siamese cat my mom had given to me almost twenty years earlier was dying. She said my mom would be there to welcome Suki into her arms. This gave me more comfort than you can imagine. I was certain that it was my mom Debbie contacted. Moreover, I was reassured knowing she would welcome the cat she had blessed me with. I am so grateful.

~Caron Allen Taira,
daughter of Marcia Mazur Gold

<u>Lalo Ernesto Castro</u>

(December 31, 1975 to November 24, 2004)
Watsonville, California

During my reading, Debbie mentioned Lalo's favorite pens were Paper
Mate. Debbie mentioned that while she was talking with me none of
her pens would work. This made no sense until she shared the type of
pen it was. Because Lalo was a writer, he never used anything else but
this type of pen.

My father was a heavy smoker. He smoked cigars and Lucky Strike cigarettes every day. Lalo looked like my father, but was not as aggressive personality-wise. Debbie mentioned in the reading that someone helped Lalo cross over. She said it was someone who smoked. At first, I could not think of who it was, but then she said, "You would smell the smoke." I said, "I would not smell the smoke because I cannot smell." Debbie replied, "You will." That was true three or four times when I was sad about Lalo, because smoke started to fill my nose. It was not unpleasant, but just my dad. I know he loved Lalo. My dad was a firefighter for over twenty-five years. If anyone had gone to get Lalo, to rescue him from the unknown, it would have been by dad, William "Bill" Doerr.

In July 2004, Lalo bought his sister Sunny a 2005 Scion TC Toyota, a fast little car. He never had a credit card or a car that he paid off. Because he was going to get married and we agreed to give him the money to get a house, he wanted to establish credit for himself. That was why he purchased the car for Sunny. On August 18, 2004, a truck driver rammed the car. Sunny did not want to call Lalo and tell him the car she was driving—the car that was in his name—had been crushed. She said over and over, "but it was not my fault." Lalo only asked how she was. He later made fun of her. "Drive slow," he would say. She would say back, "It wasn't my fault." He would reply, "Right!" The following October, he bought Sunny another Scion TC Toyota and told her, "Drive slow." She said back, "It wasn't my fault." He replied laughing, "Right!"

He loved his little sister and did not want the car he bought for her to be something she would be injured in. That is why during the reading when I asked if he had anything to say to Sunny, he mentioned the car. "Drive slow" he said, but Sunny still says, "But it wasn't my fault!" We can still hear Lalo's laugh saying…"Right!"

~Barbara Castro,
mother of Lalo Castro

SABRA ARMINDA "MINNIE" ADAMS

(March 27, 1898 to May 9, 1985)
Johnstown, Ohio

This is my grandma, "Minnie." I knew that it was my grandma when Debbie said that she was very neat and organized—and I was too. I also knew that she would mention my father (her son) whom I have not seen for many years and who is probably going to pass over sometime soon. She wanted me to know that if I saw him again, the look in his eyes would be of love and not rejection. She also expressed concern about my daughter's nanny, and I later found out that my daughter was not as happy as she appeared. Thanks so much for re-connecting me with her.

~Diane Powell,
granddaughter of Minnie Adams

Joyce and Julie

Joyce Beischel

(May 18, 1945 to September 28, 1999)
Fountain Hills, Arizona

My encounters with my mom through Debra have really encouraged my understanding of her continued presence in my life.

~Dr. Julie Beischel,
daughter of Joyce Beischel

Ted Alfred Hermes

(February 14, 1982 to August 22, 1999)
Mesa, Arizona

Just before my daughter and I left our home with the grim task of picking out a plot for Ted, she hugged me and said she really did not know what to do. I told her I did not know either, and then a voice inside me told her, "Maybe there will be a yellow butterfly?" I had no idea where that came from or why I said it.

At the cemetery, a yellow butterfly landed under a tree where we were looking. We chose that spot. We never take these occurrences for granted anymore or blow them off as a coincidence. Instead, I embrace them in my heart with the warmth from his spirit. I now see many yellow butterflies.

I will always be grateful to Debbie, especially the day she called me about the garbage. It was a Wednesday morning, and I was at work. I was still struggling pretty badly with not knowing how to accept his loss. That morning was "garbage day," and I opened the lid and saw what Ted had spray-painted on the inside of the lid, "Feed me." Instead of feeling sad, I smiled remembering what a goof ball he was and how he always made me smile. I felt a warmth in my heart as if he was there chuckling too. When Debbie called me later that morning and said, "I don't know why, but I need to tell you something about your garbage." Ted's presence was with Debbie that morning. He told her that he hated doing the garbage. That was another "Oh my gosh" moment, when Debbie taught me not to take these moments for granted. I have learned to cherish these moments when I feel his spirit so close. I did that morning, and Debbie confirmed it. Many blessings to you.

~Brenda Hermes,
mother of Ted Hermes

Robert James Satzinger

(July 4, 1918 to June 1995)
Brooklyn Heights, New York

At the start of our reading, Debbie told me that my father was showing her a birthday cake. His birthday held great meaning for me. My father always gives me a sign on his birthday, the Fourth of July. It was on that day when Julia, my three-year-old, was playing. She stopped, looked up, and said, "Hi Grandpa." Alicia my two-year-old then said, "Hi Grandpa." There was silence. Julia said, "But where are you? Are you here?" Alicia answered, while looking up, "I'm here. I can see you."

On another Fourth of July, I turned off my trusty computer. Two days later the only date that would appear was the Fourth of July. I changed the master date, but no luck. I then changed it every way I could think of and re-booted it. That failed too. I kept trying, but it would only say the fourth no matter what I did.

During the reading, Debbie passed along a bit of difficult medical advice from my father. She then added, "He said, 'Sweetie...'" At first, I was confused because no one in my life uses "Sweetie." Later I remembered that we picked up using "Sweetie" and "Honey" at a bridge game as a joke when talking in a persuasive, serious manner. No one else except my father knew that, and I had forgotten.

~Winnie Schirrmeister,
daughter of Robert Satzinger

Grace Natalie Parker Vereen

(March 31, 1930 to September 13, 1985)
Perry, Florida

During my reading with my mother, she gave me some suggestions that were very relevant to me specifically. She said, "Follow your heart and your mind, and everything will be ok. Do not just follow your mind– and do not over analyze everything–it makes you worry too much."

She also made a suggestion to my sister who is an ovarian cancer survivor. She said, "Write about your experience and help others learn." My mother died from ovarian cancer and sees her death as a way that helped my sister be a survivor. If she had not had cancer and died from it, my sister may not have recognized her own symptoms and received treatment as fast as she did. Her quick actions saved her life.

During the reading, I asked my mother what her "life" was like now. She said, "All was peaceful and happy." She added, "You continue with your own personality in the afterlife." Also, in the afterlife, she viewed her "life" as one of love and lessons. She said that she was an "energy" force that could be in more than one place at a time. Thus, she could watch over her children and grandchildren.

–Therese Vereen,
daughter of Grace Vereen

ODESSA VIRGINIA WEBSTER
(February 24, 2003 to March 25, 2004)
Gainesville, Florida

At Odessa's funeral service on our family farm, we sang the first two verses of the song "You Are My Sunshine," a song I often sang to Odessa when she was alive. Odessa was our family's sunshine, and when she died, our sun went out.

Odessa disagrees. She told me, through Debbie, to look at the abundant blooms in her memorial garden at our home as proof that her sun still shines upon us. Odessa said she showers the plants with kisses to make them grow—and grow they do, heavy with blossoms and butterflies.

For Odessa's first birthday, I wanted to buy her a "lovey." After sorting through mounds of plush teddies, bunnies, puppies, and kitties, I settled on a red-haired monkey. Now this, I thought, suits my spirited, busy daughter! "Monk Monk," as he came to be called, was a hit. She toddled everywhere with Monk in tow.

After Odessa died, Monk—and monkeys in general—became Odessa's spiritual representative. We began to collect monkey bookmarks, socks, t-shirts—anything that provided us with a tangible connection to her.

With her memorial fund, we adopted the Capuchin Monkey Habitat at Santa Fe Community College, the local college where I was employed and whose faculty and staff had been so supportive of me and my family in our grief.

Friends and family also began associating monkeys with Odessa and would share "monkey stories" with us when they seemed to be messages from our girl. One such story involves the daughter of Debbie, whose blond, bright-eyed appearance reminds me of Odessa herself. According to Debbie, her daughter called her attention during a swim lesson as the little girl demonstrated a new skill. "Look Mom," she said, as she scooted down the pool wall, one hand over the other, "I'm doing the monkey dance!" Debbie said the term came not from the swim coach, but from her daughter herself. She thought of Odessa.

Odessa loved to dance, which for her consisted of bobbing up and down to the music's rhythm by bending her knees, but we never used the term "monkey dance" when she was alive.

The term "monkey dance" came up again a few months later, this time from one of Odessa's former playgroup friends. The mother told me that her daughter Emma, who had a photo of Odessa and Monk hanging in her room, started doing what Emma called the monkey dance. She videotaped Emma doing the dance to share it with me since she immediately thought of Odessa.

In a reading with Debbie months later, I mentioned my idea of donating plush monkeys to the children displaced by Hurricane Katrina and asked Odessa what she thought of it. Debbie described the plush monkey Odessa was showing her: long legs and long arms that swung about when shaken. Odessa was calling it "the monkey dance"! Debbie's description fit Odessa's Monk perfectly, and the "monkey dance," as Odessa described it, was exactly what we did with Monk when playing with Odessa's baby sister, Arabella. I had never put the two together.

Apparently, Odessa decided to elaborate on her spiritual representative and put him into action—the only state of being that Odessa herself knew!

~Anita Webster,
Odessa's mother

Carol Elizabeth Kinter

(June 29, 1967 to February 7, 2004)
San Diego, California

The most personally meaningful message that Carol communicated through Debbie was the following: "Nothing has changed in who I am. I understand why my life was short. I am happy. So happy!" When I asked if there was anything we, her family, could do to help her in any way, Debbie said, "Keep her memory alive. Remember the good things. Show who she was and what her life represented. Feel her presence."

~Laura Hilton,
sister of Carol Kinter

The McCaul Family

Miriam Francis McCaul, "Corky"

(April 7, 1921 to July 24, 1983)
Fargo, North Dakota

Delbert Bell McCaul, "Del"

(March 1, 1918 to September 2, 1977)
Fargo, North Dakota

Brian Anthony McCaul

(March 12, 1947 to October 7, 1973)
Fargo, North Dakota

During the reading, Debbie said my father Del and my mother Corky were standing together. She asked, "Who is Daisy?" I replied that Daisy was my father's dog and was very loyal and much loved. Debbie said that Daisy was with them. It was also said during the reading that my father was in the market trying to get me to buy some potato chips. My father loved potato chips. My father also stated that he liked my husband and friends that I have in my life.

My brother Brian McCaul was a Deputy Sheriff and was killed by a drunk driver when he was twenty-six years old. Debbie told me he rides with me in the car, guides, and protects me. I always call upon him when I feel I need the help. He and my father shared a similar sense of humor, and they were a lot of fun. Their personalities came alive during the reading. Since Debbie told me about my brother's presence in my car, I feel much safer because I can feel him.

My mother Miriam was artistic and reserved. She told Debbie that she still bosses me around, telling me what to do. That was why I often forget what I was doing and would start something else. This was very true. Debbie also saw a woman that stands on my right by the name of Ellen or Helen. It was my grandmother, Helen.

The numbers 11:11 always happen when my kids and I are together. While I was in California, I waited in the car for my daughter. I sat in the backseat with the ignition off. My daughter was in a studio making a commercial for a local radio station. After she finished, we planned to go to the cemetery to pay our respects to my mother, father, and brother. When the rear windshield wipers came on, it was exactly 11:11 a.m. Debbie told me that my brother Brian was the one who was with me in the car looking after my safety and wanted me to acknowledge him more often. I really do feel him around me more than before. This was just another verification that my brother Brian was with me that day. The sequence of the number "ones" represented my loved ones, letting me know they were around. So now, when I see this, I say, "Hi guys, what's up?"

During the reading, Debbie told me that my father would come to my daughter in a courtyard. She had just bought a house, and no one else knew about it yet. It had a courtyard. My daughter now sits out in that courtyard and visits with her grandfather. She gets a great deal of comfort from sitting there when she has troubles. I say to him, "Thanks for helping her."

Since my reading with Debbie, I have felt a real sense of peace and knowledge that one day I will be reunited with my family.

~Robin Campbell,
daughter of Del and Corky McCaul
and sister of Brian McCaul

Warren Arthur Sather

(May 9, 1927 to February 2, 2000)
Chandler, Arizona

Warren Arthur Sather lived in Chicago as a child and then moved to Warrenville, Illinois, but had a business in Glen Ellyn, Illinois as a barber for twenty-eight years. He then retired and moved to Chandler, Arizona where he lived and ran a motel for 26 years. He was, and is, a very kind and compassionate man. He was very generous and had a lot of courage. His family was everything to him.

Warren's daughters, with their families and his wife, gathered for a reading to hear messages from their father and husband. This man left a legacy–he left a family filled with unconditional love for Warren Sather. It is a love that will never disappear, but will only continue to grow from generation to generation

The reading, or experience, we had with Debbie was a great reward for my whole family. It gave us all a great sense of peace knowing that my dad is around us and watching over all of us. Our family sighted examples of messages that my dad said to each one of us, which were wonderful gifts. For me, it was his approval and encouragement to make great changes in my life. Just to know that he was with me and saw all that was happening, and welcomed the changes for me was my gift.

For my mother it was great comfort to see the hummingbird around her house. It reassured her that he was close by and made her heart sing. During the reading, my father stated that he sends hummingbirds to let her know that he was close by.

Since the reading, my sister has been able to quiet herself enough to be able to hear him speak to her. She, in turn, uses her gift to ask about her children's life path and about the rest of us. My dad's thoughts are with us.

I could list many things that were said during the reading that gave my family validation this was my father. But all in all, I think the greatest thing was the assurance that even though he was not here in the flesh, he made his spirit known to us. It was wonderful to know he was not far away and was looking out for us just like he protected us when he was here on earth.

~Donna Miller,
daughter of Warren Sather

ENDNOTES

[1] VERITAS Research Program, Gary E. Schwartz, University of Arizona, www.veritas.arizona.edu.

[2] Wendy Orr, *Arabella* (Australia: Angus & Robertson, 1998).

[3] Doreen Virtue, *Angel Therapy* (Carlsbad, CA: Hay House, Inc., 1997).

[4] Gary E. Schwartz with William L. Simon, *The Afterlife Experiments* (New York, NY: Simon & Schuster, Inc., 2002).

[5] Susy Smith, *The Afterlife Codes* (Charlottesville, VA: Hampton Roads Publishing Company, 2000).

[6] For further information, refer to www.veritas.arizona.edu.

[7] Gary E. Schwartz, *The Truth about Medium* (Charlottesville, VA: Hampton Roads, 2005).

[8] Hazel Courteney, *The Evidence for the Sixth Sense* (London, England: Cico Books, 2005).

[9] Gary E. Schwartz, *Mediums: We See Dead People*, The Arts and Entertainment Network, original air date October 14, 2005.

[10] Please refer http://veritas.arizona.edu/rsmediums.htm for the complete document. The purpose of this document is to describe the opportunities, responsibilities, and requirements for Mediums

and researchers involved in integrative mediumship research with the VERITAS Research Program.

[11] Schwartz, *The Afterlife Experiments.*

[12] Schwartz, *The Truth about Medium.*

[13] Ibid., 70.

[14] Susy Smith, *Ghost Writers in the Sky: More Communication from James* (Lincoln, NE: iUniverse, Inc., 1990).

[15] Ibid, 45-46.

[16] Schwartz, *The Afterlife Experiments*, 237-238.

[17] Ibid.

ACKNOWLEDGEMENTS

To **Dr. Julie Beischel**, my business took off the day we met. You truly believed in me, and without you, all of this may never have happened. I have enjoyed all of the experiments and challenges you have presented to me. I consider you more than a colleague; you are a treasured friend. I also appreciate the time you take to assist me whenever I ask. I feel blessed that I can share anything with you and count on you for guidance.

My deepest gratitude goes to **Dr. Gary Schwartz** whom I highly respect and honor. He is a professor at the University of Arizona and founded its Human Energy Systems Laboratory. Thank you for sharing with me concrete evidence that validates the words I receive from spirits are accurate and compelling. Your support has given me the credentials, and more importantly, the confidence to share my gift with others. I am immensely grateful for the friendship and trust we have developed through the years. Finally, I am deeply honored and thrilled that you wrote the Foreword for my book. I can only hope that I will make you proud.

To **Susy Smith**, you have been my steadfast guide to Dr. Julie Beischel and Dr. Gary Schwartz. Without your unrelenting encouragement, I may have given up easily and never met these two incredible experts. Everything you have done for me, including this book cover, has been a true miracle! I sincerely thank you.

To **Michelle Madruga**, thank you for being my writing partner and for making the process of completing my manuscript pain-free and fun. Though the content of this book primarily comes from me, the polishing of my words to make them clearer than I could is your hard work. You asked me probing questions and then connected and understood the spirit of my words perfectly. You helped me make my book everything I hoped it would be. I am grateful for the box in your entry hall that one particular day—the contents forever changed the depth of our friendship.

To my husband, **Ric**, without your believing in me, I would not have accomplished all that I have. You are the blessing that walked into my life at just the right time. You are my knight in shining armor. Your calm patience, unconditional love, and unwavering support have truly kept me balanced while writing this book over the past year. Thank you for all that you are and for all that you have done.

To my son, **Steven**, thank you for believing in me and not being afraid to share my gift with your friends.

To my daughter, **Stephanie**, thank you for accepting and understanding my abilities.

To my son, **Brad**, because you also have the ability to see the spirits, I believe that we share a special bond. Thank you for being the model on my book cover.

To my daughter, **Allison**, thank you for being such a patient little girl by giving me the time I needed to dedicate to this book.

To my parents, **Frank and Delores Puehringer**, thank you for guiding me through this journey. I love you.

To my sister, **Cindy Francione**, thank you for respecting my gift and for seeing and sharing our parents' signs together. You are not only my sister, but also my best friend.

To my sister, **Linda Gustavson**, although we may believe in different ways, our common threads are our friendship and sisterhood. I love you for that.

To **Grandpa and Grandma Martin**, thank you for your support and love in making my dream come true.

To **Grandma and Grandpa Russell**, thank you for believing in me and watching this all transpire.

To my dear friend, **Jan Moffitt**, thank you for all of the evenings spent at your house meditating. You inspired me to write this book. You are a woman who always writes with perfect words. I thank you for your trust and belief in me.

To **Sheri Roach**, thank you for always having the right contacts and asking nothing in return.

To my dear friend, **Chris Loo**, thank you for allowing me to be present at the passing of your grandfather. It revealed death in another light for me.

To my assistant and friend, **Kristina Moffitt**, thank you for being with me day in and day out. You have witnessed every thought and event that has taken place during the process of writing this book. Thank you for always listening.

To **Ray Madruga,** I cannot wait to hear your review of this book and if you are open to becoming a believer. Thank you, too, for your patient hours while your wife and I perfected this book.

To **Allison Robinson**, thank you for your generous time and words of wisdom. You helped put the finishing touches on my book.

Thank you, **Lee Ann Morlan**, for always speaking from your heart. You will always be a treasured friend.

Thank you, **Rollie Zagnoli**, for being open-minded and for supporting my husband during this journey. To Sally Zagnoli, how our lives changed in one day with all of the experiences we shared together. More importantly, it is all with such joy and love. What a treasure we received from your father. Absence truly makes the heart grow fonder.

To **Don Hoey**, I will be forever grateful to you for giving me the book *The Afterlife Experiments* by Dr. Gary Schwartz.

Thank you, **Anita Webster**, for allowing and trusting in me to be the link between you and your daughter, Odessa. In addition, thank you for helping me share your story in Chapter One. I give my heartfelt thanks to you in making this chapter such a special introduction to this book.

To **Odessa Webster**, you are a child that I look forward to meeting when I cross over. You gave me the gift of understanding what parents are looking for when they lose a child.

To **Dick Mitchell**, thank you for trusting in me as a medium. We continue to share a spiritual connection that no one else understands.

To Dick Mitchell's daughters, **Tinley and Debbie**, thank you for allowing me to share your father's story and be present in his last moments.

To **Dale and Karen Fischer**, thank you for making my connection with Dick Mitchell possible and for becoming my friends.

Thank you, **Marcy Smith**, for sharing the signs you received during a reading, which later became evident.

Thank you, **Teresa, Eric, Chase, and Benton Seyler**, for trusting in my abilities and sharing them with others.

To **Katie Zurich**, her son Andrew, **Helene Carroll**, and her son Dustin, thank you for letting me share your story. May we continue being friends.

To **Judy and John Peters**, thank you for sharing your abilities as holistic, hypnosis, energy healers. May your energy now shine through from the afterlife.

To **Becky Feola** and her beloved husband Neil, thank you for teaching me life is not over when one contracts a deadly disease.

To **Albert Manjarrez**, thank you for allowing me, the angels, the guides, and the Highest Divine heal you.

To Karyl and Mike O'Leary, thank you for our new friendship that was created after a reading about your son Ken. I look forward to the key chains and bookmarks you offered to create for others to purchase on my website. More importantly, thank you for the use of your words at the end of my book. They are beautifully written and the perfect way to end my story.

To **Janis Klein** at CBS, thank you for producing the show *Mediums: We See Dead People*. Thank you for all of your hard work in making it possible for people to observe what I do.

To **Rob Konieczny** (robkphoto@hotmail.com), thank you for designing my book cover and taking my photos.

To **Bill Lurie** of Emarketing-Canada.com, thank you for consistently updating my webpage and making it easy for my clients to find me on the Internet. Your quick response and efficiency never cease to amaze me.

To **Mark Bogan**, thank you for all of your legal advice, support, and belief in me.

To my **heavenly guides**, thank you for guiding my words and research throughout the writing of this book. I could not have done it without you.

To the **spirit world**, thank you for guiding me in the right direction, for speaking clearly when I am doing a reading, and for continuing to use me as your voice.

To my **clients**, thank you for trusting in me to contact your loved ones. Every reading has been unique and has touched my heart.

Thank you, **AuthorHouse**, for assisting me with the publication of this book.

As featured on the A&E documentary *Mediums: We See Dead People*, **Debra Martin** is a Laboratory Research Medium with the VERITAS Research Program through the University of Arizona, located in Tucson, Arizona. In addition, she has achieved recognition as a Lab Certified Medium by the Forever Family Foundation, Inc. based in Oceanside, New York. Debra resides in Phoenix, Arizona with her husband and four children. Please visit her website at www.goldenmiracles.com.

Writing partner, **Michelle G. Madruga,** is a graduate of Claremont McKenna College. Although this is her first experience with the publication of a book, her twelve years of commercial banking experience plus her love of writing provided her with a solid foundation for this endeavor. She and her husband reside in Northern California with their two children.

Printed in the United States
68070LVS00009B/130